"Brilliant, well-researched, laugh-out-loud funny and empowering. Ed Drew is the perfect companion (ally, teacher, confidante and friend) for the crazy roller coaster that we call parenting."

JONTY AND LINDA ALLCOCK, The Globe Church, London

"Our children are growing up in a very different world to the one we grew up in, and there are certain conversations we can dread as parents! Thank you, Ed, for this book and for not shying away from the hot topics but offering practical insights on how parents can navigate the big questions of the day."

ANDY FROST, Share Jesus International

"It's been said that parenthood is sanctifying. I would add that it is also often downright paralyzing. Of course, it's one of life's greatest joys too. We who are parents and also Christ-followers want to get it just right. Ed Drew writes as a friend, a fellow parent and an experienced youth minister, who clearly loves Jesus and loves kids. This book is chock-full of anecdotes and practical ideas, of Scripture and reminders of God's character, and of grace and truth. I'm so glad to have read it, and I heartily recommend it to all parents and anyone who loves children and teens."

JEN OSHMAN, Author, *Welcome; Cultural Counterfeits;* and *Enough about Me*

"No Christian should be allowed to have children without first being inspired and equipped by this wonderfully realistic and practical book!"

ED SHAW, Ministry Director, livingout.org; Author, *Purposeful Sexuality*

"This book is a must-read for every parent wanting to parent their child to navigate this life in light of eternity. Ed tackles some of the most pressing issues that parents face today with biblical insight and wisdom, and humour along the way. You may not agree with everything written in this book, but this book will prepare every parent to address pressing issues such as identity, friendships, gender, sexuality and marriage, with their child."

SANDY GALEA, Kidswise Director, Fellowship Dubai

"In this helpful book, Ed bares his heart's desire that children (not only his own) should learn that 'in God we have an unshifting solid and secure foundation on which to build our lives'. With helpful anecdotes, he supports parents as they deal with some of the issues of identity that children and especially teenagers face in our current fast-changing culture. By taking every opportunity for communication with our children, we are encouraged to show that, as Ed says, they are 'made by a great God and loved by a great Saviour'."

DR LIZ JONES, Lovewise; Author, *Growing Up God's Way*; Retired Paediatrician

"There are so many reasons to love this book. It takes complicated Bible truths and applies them to the nitty-gritty of everyday parenting. It tackles the hardest and most confusing contemporary challenges and responds with measured, biblical wisdom. Filled with real-life stories that are told with insight and compassion (and much delightful humour), Ed Drew's book is for parents who want to help their children build an identity in which confidence is rooted not in themselves but in the God who created them and the Saviour who came to redeem them."

STEVE MIDGLEY, Executive Director, Biblical Counselling UK; Author, *Mental Health and Your Church*

"Highly readable, this book is biblical but also honest about the modern challenges to modern parents. It is encouraging, challenging and comforting. It deals with godly and wise principles rather than detailed practical tips, and the chapters on gender and sexuality are a must."

DEBBIE HARDYMAN, Missionary; Special-Needs Dentist

"This book has achieved the rare thing of genuinely impacting my day-to-day practice as a parent. Ed Drew well illustrates the need in this cultural moment for parenting that moves beyond our basic protective instincts to build Christ-centred confidence and resilience in our kids. The gospel offers children resources and power to navigate the inevitable suffering and confusion that life holds—our parenting can bear witness to this!"

RACHEL WILSON, Author, *The Life We Never Expected*

"This book offers parents a perfect (and rare) combination of biblical philosophy and present day practicality. Ed Drew relays the truth of Scripture in a way that filled my heart with affection for Christ, compassion for my children and gratitude for my own identity. He addresses the issues facing today's kids with specificity, delicacy, courage and confidence, and he has left me feeling equipped to do the same. I laughed, cried, and whispered sincere thank-yous as I read. Words from this book are already taped to my mirror, shaping my responses to my kids and permeating my conversations with friends. I will return to its wisdom again and again."

ABBEY WEDGEWORTH, Author, the *Training Young Hearts* series and *Held*

RAISING CONFIDENT KIDS

in a Confusing World

ED DREW

With thanks to...

Amy Smith, Cathy Dalton, Karen Sleeman, Ed Shaw,
Carl Laferton, Rachel Allord, Andrew Bunt,
Julie Maxwell, my family and a host of authors,
experts and friends who supplied me with stories,
wisdom, patience and inspiration.

The brilliance is theirs. The mistakes are all my own.

www.faithinkids.org

for more resources on identity for children and families

Raising Confident Kids in a Confusing World
© 2023 Edward Drew

Published by:
The Good Book Company

thegoodbook.com | thegoodbook.co.uk
thegoodbook.com.au | thegoodbook.co.nz | thegoodbook.co.in

ISBN: 9781784988678 | Printed in the UK

Cover design by Drew McCall

CONTENTS

If you're reading this and you are American, I have a confession to make: I'm British. Which means (among other things) that I grew up with a mum not a mom, changed nappies and not diapers when my kids were little, and talk about secondary school and not high school. I am sure that in the pages that follow, there will be a heap of spellings that look wrong to you, some phrases that sound a bit unfamiliar, and a few places where you'll need to translate a bit for your own context. But I'm also sure that our cultures are, in the main, not very dissimilar, that children are children wherever you live, and that the gospel is wonderful and can help and inform all our parenting.

So, every time you come across something that sounds odd, I apologise—I mean, apologize. Because saying sorry is one thing that British people excel at.

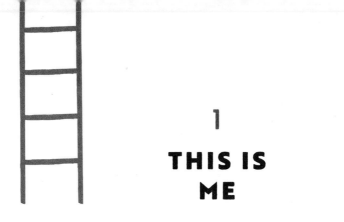

1
THIS IS ME

There are only three certainties in life: death, taxes and pictures on social media of children standing on their doorstep at the start of each new school year. My wife can't help herself. She will line our three kids up in height order, seeking to recreate the same pose she's taken every year for six years. She will ask for smiles. My daughter, aged 15, will *choose* to smile. Easy. My older son, 12, now understands that smiling will make his mother happy. That's progress. My younger son, 8, usually needs paying with a large quantity of chocolate to force a smile out of him. Some years he responds to pleading.

For our family, the whole thing is a ritual—predictable, inevitable and reassuring. A year older. A year taller. It is a snapshot of a moment in the story of our family. It is the photo we share because it is another milestone, it has the sparkly sheen of a happy family and it speaks of hope at the start of another year. This is the picture of our family that we want everyone to see. This is us. Isn't it?

JUST A DAD IN CARGO SHORTS

All of us are constantly, if not consciously, answering the question: who am I? It's the question of identity. We approach the question in different ways and come up with different answers. But it's there for all of us. Your kids are answering it. And so are you.

Personally, I have for years been proud of being a man who doesn't go in for brands or logos and who dresses unconventionally because I'm confident in being me. I think of myself as a man who stands bravely in the face of the marketing monster. I defy description. I occupy a space outside of fashion. In this sense, I am what I wear (to steal the title of a UK TV show from a couple of decades ago). My cargo shorts tell you that I am a free man. This is me!

But a few years ago I went to a U2 stadium concert. The day after, a meme went around entitled "Seating plan for U2's performance". Different areas of the stadium seating were shaded different colours, with a key underneath. Some seats were marked as "IT managers on a team-bonding offsite trip"; others as "People calling their babysitter to ask them for another two hours". I checked where I had sat. The label for my area said, "Dads in cargo shorts". I thought back. I had been wearing cargo shorts. Turns out I do not defy convention. I am the stereotype of a middle-aged man who *thinks* he defies convention.

I want to be unique. I want to be different. I want to baffle categories and conventions. But really, I don't. Who am I?

I heard recently of a teenager saying to a teacher who she trusted that she didn't know who she was. She had realised that she was a totally different person depending on whether she was with her parents or with one group of friends or another group. "Who am I?" she asked. *Which is the real me?* How can she tell?

I know several children who seem to have no friends at school. I know as a parent how it feels to ache with your child as they explain what it's like to wander around the playground alone. I remember the first child I knew who felt like that. She was 8 years old, and I thought she was a great 8-year-old. If I'd been 8, I'd have wanted to be her friend. But it turned out that all the real 8-year-olds she knew did not see it like that. I remember thinking, when I was told about her experience, "What? But she is the loveliest child! Why doesn't everyone want to be her friend?" Is this who she is? Lonely. Friendless. Isolated.

That girl is now in her mid 20s. The last time I heard, she was visiting New York with friends. Is she still the same person? Is she defined by how many friends she had aged 8? Is she worth more now that she has tons of friends?

THIS IS ME?

There is an incredibly powerful song in the movie *The Greatest Showman* called, "This is me." It is sung by the cast of Barnum's Circus. Audiences come to see them because each is in some way a "freak", but together they are a tight-knit family. Against the finger-pointing and the pity, they sing together "This is me". Their lives have been defined by rejection because of what they look like, whether it be their extreme height (or lack of it), their impressive beard (on a woman), their birthmarks or their tattoos. They sing their story: "Hide away, they say, because we don't want your broken parts. Run away, they say, no one will love you as you are."

They are defined by what they look like. Their value can be measured by the money they bring in. They are known by their defining feature—"The bearded lady" and "dwarf man" and so on. This is who they are. At least, that is what others say.

But they sing a different story. They sing of being brave as well as bruised. They sing of marching to the beat that they themselves are banging out. They sing of making no apologies for who they are. It is their angry answer to the question "Who are you?" They refuse to be the labels others give them. While they might be bruised and hurt by how they have been treated, they know that they are more than a physical quirk or an outlier from the norm.

There's something wonderful about that. There's something here that we want our own kids to emulate: to refuse to be defined by how others view them or treat them. And yet, there's something dangerous here too.

There is a spirit of our age that tells our children to give their own angry answer. Our children are being asked to start from a blank sheet of paper. Who are you? Who do you want to be? What is your gender? What is your sexuality? Where is your value? How will you be famous? What difference will you make? Follow your own path. Create your own path. Follow your heart. Be the person you want to be. Stand up and declare, without apology, "This is me".

That is not freedom, though. That is a burden. Not only that, it is shifting. What if the me I am today is not the me I was yesterday? What if I don't much like the me I am today? What if what I think and how I feel don't match up at the moment? What if the me I want to be causes hurt to the you you want to be? Creating your own identity is elusive, and it is exhausting. It leads away from confidence and towards crisis.

That spirit of the age sounds so appealing. It may even seem loving. But it is not true. Our children's hearts are at risk. We might feel overwhelmed, confused and tempted to just give in. On the other hand, we might feel fearful and hear ourselves responding negatively to the world's message by pointing out to our kids at every single opportunity—as it comes through the words of their teachers, their friends and themselves—where it is wrong.

But we have a better story to tell: one of redemption, hope and purpose. We have the best, most uplifting story to give to our children.

A CONFIDENT SHEEP

The better story is that they have been created in their Maker's image. Their loving heavenly Father has already said who they are. The Bible story tells them the truth. They can find out who they were made to be, who they are and who they will be. Once they understand, they can live free. They can make better decisions. They can be more confident. And, crucially, they can feel better.

As Christians, we are not defined by our appearances.

We are not a collection of logos and brands. We are not our hairstyle, weight or disability. We are not the names we are called. We are not what other people see of us. As the prophet Samuel came to find the boy who would be the greatest king of the Old Testament, he was reminded that this was not going to be an orchestrated Instagram moment:

> But the LORD said to Samuel, "Do not consider his appearance or his height, for I have rejected him. The LORD does not look at the things people look at. People look at the outward appearance, but the LORD looks at the heart." (1 Samuel 16:7)

So it was that God chose a shepherd-boy, David, to be king of his people. And that shepherd-king pointed forwards to *the* Shepherd-King, the Lord Jesus, who promised:

> The thief comes only to steal and kill and destroy; I have come that they may have life, and have it to the full. I am the good shepherd. The good shepherd lays down his life for the sheep. (John 10:10-11)

Jesus' words here have all the emotional uplift of a Hollywood blockbuster. Hear the feel-good story. Listen to the promise of life to the full. Which parent does not want that for their children? This is our universal desire for our children. Jesus Christ claimed that it was found in him, as the good shepherd.

Others come to steal, kill and destroy life—the shepherd came to give life. He did so by laying down his life at a moment in history. This is not a trendy self-help philosophy or the latest breakthrough parenting book. This is flesh and bone. This is love and sacrifice. This is the real-life shepherd. This best life is available to "the sheep".

We are not defined by those around us. But equally, we are not a blank sheet of paper. The only answer to the question "Who am I?" that gives us a confidence and a joy and a freedom is "I am a sheep". It is the shepherd who tells us what we are and makes us what we are—at the cost of his own life.

God is a loving heavenly Father who adores your children. His children, if they live with their faith in him. He tells them, *You are precious because I made you, Your body is good because I made it* and *You have infinite value because my Son died for you.* If they know and feel God's love, they will trust and obey him more fully.

Jesus said, "If you hold to my teaching, you are really my disciples. Then you will know the truth, and the truth will set you free" (John 8:31-32).

Being a parent is a strange business. What no one can prepare you for is the emotional burden. I feel an ache for my children, particularly when they feel broken, that compares to nothing else. When Jesus says that he knows the way for *my children* to be set free and to enjoy life to the full, I am all ears. I am all in. I think I am more engaged than when I think about the freedom that he has given *me*. To be a parent is to frequently find yourself putting your own freedom to one side for the sake of your children's. In my better moments, I am clear that my children will probably be my most significant legacy. I would choose to have achieved nothing with my life if they could be truly free.

I trust Jesus. He offers them freedom. When they are asked, "Who are you?" before all else, I want them to stand tall, to puff out their chests and to say in a clear, confident voice, "I am a disciple of Jesus. *This is me.*"

I want them, on their worst days, to remember that Jesus loves them and that that's ultimately all that matters. I want them, on their best days, to remember that Jesus loves them and that that's what matters most. I want them to meet with triumph and despair and treat both those experiences with the confidence that comes from knowing in their hearts that who they are, and who they will always be, is greatly loved children of a heavenly Father. Because if that is their identity, then they will navigate a confusing world, and walk towards an eternal home, with confidence.

THE SECOND SUNDAY

Parenting in our house seems mostly to be spent shouting the word "Shoes", wondering how many screens are currently scattered throughout our home, and wishing that we carved out more of that mythical "quality family time" that we hear spoken of by people whose surname is not Drew.

But one day there will only be two pairs of shoes to find (and my wife is very good at sorting her own out), I will know where the screens are, and quality family time will require our adult kids to come back for the weekend.

One day, our kids will not be here. And we parent for the day when we are not there. That will be when our parenting counts. The goal of our conversations, all our prodding, all our rules and all our praise is to prepare them for when they do it all without us.

I think about the second Sunday after my children have left home. I don't know where they will be living or why they will be there, but I suspect I will have helped them move there. Perhaps it will be in a place not far from us; maybe it will be at the other end of the country. Either way, they will be making their own decisions, and I won't know about many, if any, of them. On the first Sunday, they might well take themselves to church. It is what they have always done up until that point, so perhaps just the routine will take them along. When they get there, they may well know no one at all. It is going to be a shock. So many thoughts might be racing around their minds: "Who do I sit next to?", "Is it always like this?", "Do I *want* to come back *here*?" and "No one will notice if I don't come back".

So the second Sunday is going to be a significant moment. "Do I go back to that church? Do I go back to *any* church?" When something is new, different and probably difficult, you need something more than a well-worn routine. You need an identity. On that second Sunday, my kids, and your kids, need to be certain that church is part of who they are: that Jesus Christ and his people are part of the fabric of their identity.

That's what this book is about. It doesn't contain loads of surefire tactics for turning out super-happy kids. (If that's what you were hoping for, there are other books you can get that offer you those—personally I think they're over-promising and under-delivering.) I'm not going to suggest that I know all the answers. (Most days, I don't even know all the questions.) But we will be thinking: What does it look like to raise our kids to be confident in who they are, because they know whose they are? How do we parent in a way that points them to how God sees them as the fundamental basis of everything they are and do? Of course, it is God's grace and not our parenting that saves and changes our kids. But God tends to work through means, so what can you do now to prepare your kids to go to church with a song in their hearts on that second Sunday?

CULTURE > STRATEGY

There is a corporate saying: "Culture eats strategy for breakfast." It is a warning to companies to beware thinking that a printed strategy with clear goals, new meetings and revised structures will change their future. It doesn't matter how many posters are placed on the wall with defined targets and catchy soundbites; if the culture of the organisation is disengaged, cynical or demotivated, growth will not happen. To bring about change, it is always the culture that needs to be worked on. Leaders need to be talking about the strategy in a way that shows that they actually care about it, and everyone needs to be helped to see how their daily work is affected.

It is the same with parenting.

Your children live and breathe your family culture. They notice what you usually say in a crisis. They notice who you go to with your problems. They notice what gets the best of your time, what gets cancelled, what makes you angry and what makes you leap off the sofa with joy. They know what must never be interrupted and what competes for your attention. They know what goes on behind the front door in front of which you take the start-of-year photo.

That's challenging. But remember who you are: you are a sheep with a Shepherd, a child with a heavenly Father. You're not alone in your parenting. There's grace which can cover your failings and there's the Holy Spirit who can change you. Your family culture can increasingly reflect Jesus' lordship over you. Your parenting can increasingly reflect the Shepherd's love for you. This is a confusing world, for kids and for their parents. There's nothing like parenting to humble us. But that's ok—in Jesus, we have everything we need to raise confident kids. Keep going. He has you. You are his. This is who you are.

Questions to think about...

1. *Who are you?* How would you answer that question? What difference does being a follower of Christ make to your sense of identity?

2. Can you see a difference over your years as a Christian (if it has been years!) in terms of how you think about yourself, how you talk about yourself, and where your sense of peace comes from?

3. What do you think your child(ren) would say if you asked them to describe who they are?

4. In times of difficulty, who do they speak to and what do they do? When they feel unsettled or insecure, what activity or place would provide comfort and security?

There is not one right answer to these questions. Step back from your family and look at what takes the best of your time and a big chunk of your enthusiasm and money.

2

WHAT DO YOU (REALLY) WANT MOST FOR YOUR KIDS?

I am tall. Years ago, I discovered that my thigh bone is in the longest 1% of all femurs. When I meet in the flesh people with whom I've had multiple conversations on Zoom, they almost always say, "You are very tall!" (I haven't yet found a good reply: "Yes I am" feels a bit bland, but "I have a top-1% femur" is a little geeky.) I have regularly heard myself described as "the tall one." My height is apparently the most noticeable thing about me.

There was a song we used to sing in Sunday school that began, "Zacchaeus was a very little man; and a very little man was he". Two thousand years after he made it into a Gospel, his lack of height is the one thing that thousands of children know about him. I think Zacchaeus would be relieved that we're singing about his height. In his day, as he walked down the streets of Jericho, the children would have been singing something very different: "Zacchaeus is filthy traitor scum; and filthy traitor scum is he" does not scan, but it would be closer to the mark.

Yes, Zacchaeus was short—but he was also a chief tax collector (Luke 19:2-3). His community would have cared more about his job than his height. To be a tax collector meant working for the despised occupying force, the Romans. The job of the tax collector was to take money from your own Jewish community and give it to the Roman occupiers. (Imagine a Ukrainian putting his hand up to be a tax collector for the Russian army.) Worse, tax collectors didn't get a salary, so they added to the taxes to make their own profits. The Romans didn't care if the Jews were ripped off so that their tax collectors could get rich. Zacchaeus was not just a tax collector but the chief. He would skim off a profit from all the tax collectors' gains. Zacchaeus would have been noticeably, offensively wealthy, and it was all gained from being a collaborator. Everyone knew him. And everyone hated him.

If you had asked someone in Jericho to line up their community with "good" people at one end and "bad" at the other, Zacchaeus would have been stood on his own at the far bad end. You and I would have thoroughly agreed with their assessment. Zacchaeus had an identity. It defined him. This was who he was.

THE RELIGIOUS MISTAKE

Have you seen what children do when they want to be picked by a teacher? They do this thing where they cross their arms, sit bolt upright, open their eyes wide, hold their breath and sit statue-still. The teacher has to pick quickly or lives could be lost. I imagine an adult version of that when Jesus walked through the crowd as he passed through Jericho, searching for a host for his afternoon tea. Every adult was quietly murmuring on repeat, "Pick me. Pick me. Pick me." Perhaps they didn't even notice the short, hated collaborator climbing a tree so that he could see Jesus as he walked by.

After all, if Jesus was going to choose one person to have a cup of tea and piece of cake with, then surely he would choose anyone, absolutely anyone, except Zacchaeus the chief tax collector.

> When Jesus reached the spot, he looked up and said to him, "Zacchaeus, come down immediately. I must stay at your house today." (v 5)

Oh no! the whole crowd exhale as one. Who is going to tell Jesus about this guy? This is so awkward. I can't actually believe he's doing this.

After the initial shock and questions have passed, the crowd's reaction changes:

> All the people saw this and began to mutter, "He has gone to be the guest of a sinner." (v 7)

This is fantastically understated. If this had happened in your community, what would all the people have said to each other, some under their breath but most so that everyone could hear? I don't dare write here what I would have said. I would have felt outraged. This is all wrong.

The crowd's reaction, and mine, is the reaction of religion.

Religion keeps the good away from the bad. The devout are kept out of reach of the immoral. Blessings are for good people, and bad people get what they deserve. This is why bullies are not invited to the parties of sweet, well-behaved children. Throughout the Gospels, it's usually the Pharisees who are the great example of this approach to life. Whenever Jesus took time to eat with the sinners, the prostitutes and the tax collectors, they would stand at a distance and mutter, just as the good people of Jericho do here. The Pharisees were the Jewish leaders who kept all the religious rules. They set the tone. And the residents of Jericho followed.

Religion makes an identity out of actions and behaviours. It prioritises the ability to say, "I am good"—and it tells us that, if we can, that's where we find confidence and security. Religion is where everyone's hearts tend to go—even those who don't think they're religious. If you keep doing the right thing because it's the right thing, and you feel pleased with yourself when you do—that's religion. If you hang around with good people, notice the failings of others in a way that makes you feel better about yourself, and make sure you don't show other people the bad things you do—that's religion.

Parenting usually takes a religious approach, even in families who don't think they're religious. We train our children to keep doing good things. We try to stop them doing bad things in front of others. (Behind closed doors, it's not so bad.) We show them how to present well to others. If we can raise our children to the point where they only do good things in front of others, then they are ready to be released into the wild, without us. That is usually the goal of most parenting. Good behaviour is what matters most.

JESUS WAS NOT RELIGIOUS

The problem with Christians parenting religiously is that Jesus Christ was not religious. He knew exactly what Zacchaeus was like—and he still chose him. Jesus knew everything Zacchaeus had ever done. He also knew why he had done it. He knew his insecurities, his anger, his hurt, his desires and his longings. Jesus was not dismissing the sin. He was not about to say that Zacchaeus was actually a good man, or that he was just misunderstood, or that it was just an issue of perspective, or that his sin wasn't his own fault. Jesus was not about to blame Zacchaeus' surroundings, his difficult upbringing, his father, or his social group. Jesus excused nothing Zacchaeus had done, and yet he still chose the worst sinner in town. Deliberately. He did it to teach the whole of Jericho a lesson. He did it to teach me a lesson. He did it to give Zacchaeus a new identity.

In our culture, we might miss the significance of the moment that Jesus went into Zacchaeus' house to eat with him. Eating in someone's house was an act of intimacy. (Perhaps in our day it would be like giving someone the keys to your home to come and go as they please.) It was a sign of deep trust and deep friendship. That is why all the people agreed that this was an outrage. Don't miss the tragic irony: as Jesus enjoys friendship with the one man who seems to have known he had a problem, all the people who assumed they were good are missing out on enjoying friendship with him. As Jesus told the Pharisees when they complained about him befriending another tax collector, Levi, "It is not the healthy who need a doctor, but those who are ill. I have not come to call the righteous, but sinners" (Mark 2:17). You need to know you're ill to visit the doctor. You need to know you're not that good to come to Jesus. That's what kept the Pharisees from Jesus: their sense of their goodness—their religion.

To this day, Jesus wants to invite himself into the lives of the worst of people. He wants to be intimate with the untouchable—whether theirs is a very visible sin, like that of Zacchaeus, or the kind that secretly sits in our hearts, which only we know about.

To this day, Jesus wants us to invite the worst of people (whatever our culture has decided constitutes the "worst") into our churches to hear the welcome that Jesus offers. This is the difference between religion and Christianity.

THE SALVATION BUSINESS

It's fine to be confused right now and to think, "But I thought Christians were meant to be good?" Let's take it one step at a time. Listen to how Jesus explained to the muttering crowds what he was up to:

> *Today salvation has come to this house, because this man, too, is a son of Abraham. For the Son of Man came to seek and to save the lost. (Luke 19:9-10)*

Jesus is in the salvation business. The "before" picture is always of someone in need of rescue. The "after" picture is always of someone in a place of safety. Being saved by Jesus means a change in identity. When Zacchaeus walked into his house with Jesus, he was counted among "the lost". No one would have disagreed with that. His behaviour was a sign that he was lost. But the language of being lost is a clue that his problem was so much more than stealing, cheating or betraying. He was lost from God. He was so far from being in relationship with him.

Notice the language of identity. Jesus came for the sick because he is the doctor. He came for the sinners and not for the righteous. What Jesus cares about is identity. Behaviour change will never be enough without a change of identity.

Jesus was clear why he came. God became a man, left heaven's throne room, and was born in a stable to... come for people like Zacchaeus—the lost. That is hard to accept. It was impossible to accept for the people of Jericho. Jesus came for me because I was lost. Jesus came for you because you were lost. Jesus did not come for us because we go to church. Jesus did not come for us because we were ready and waiting. He did not come for your kids because they are well-behaved or know the answers in Sunday school. Jesus came for our children because they were lost—and might still be lost.

And when Jesus gets involved, salvation happens. He is not primarily in the business of behaviour improvement or increased church attendance (though he does a great line in both). He is in the salvation business. It's a miracle, every time it happens. I think the most shocking language in the Bible to describe the change that happens when Jesus saves is in Ephesians 2:

As for you, you were dead in your transgressions and sins ... But because of his great love for us, God, who is rich in mercy, made us alive with Christ even when we were dead in transgressions—it is by grace you have been saved.
(v 1, 4-5)

Before being saved, we were dead. Not physically dead but spiritually dead: dead to God as our Creator, dead in terms of our relationship with God. Have you ever seen a stuffed animal? A stag's head on the wall of an old building? A stuffed bear in a museum? A stuffed bird or small animal in a bric-a-brac shop? Lifeless. Without freedom. Without the ability to make a decision. Without anything except, if you don't look at all closely, the passing appearance of life. It is hard to understand that that described us, and probably still describes some of those we love. Our identity before Jesus' salvation was that we were as dead as a stuffed animal.

And now? Now, because Jesus came for us, we are alive.

My family will tell you that I regularly take them on walks that are too long. My worst failure was the time I tried to take my family to see a herd of deer on a Scottish hillside. We never got close. At its worst moment, all three of my children were crying with tiredness. A day later, we looked out of our window, and two stags were standing there eating from the bird table. They are the largest land animal in the UK and easily the most incredible creatures I have ever seen in the wild. Pure muscle. Piercing eyes that look straight through you. Calm, dignified, beauty.

Remember that stuffed stag's head on the wall? That head was once calm, dignified, beautiful, alive. We expect what's alive to pass to what's dead. That is the natural order of things. The Christian faith is the supernatural order of things. We were dead; we were stuffed animal heads on a wall. Now we are alive: running free, muscular, wild and full of energy. Thank the Lord for Christ's salvation business!

Ephesians 2 is true of our children no less than it is of us. Apart from Christ, they, like we, are spiritually dead: facing an existence without anything good. With Christ, they are spiritually alive: enjoying life now and life for ever that is free, full, secure, eternal.

If we believe this, it places all other priorities in the background. It also places all other delights and encouragements in the background.

If you're reading this book, you may well already know all this. But in the day-to-day of parenting (and all the rest of the things that make up your life), how easy it is to forget. How hard it is genuinely to remember that what matters most is that they know Jesus, and that all that the world cares about—good behaviour, good grades, good job, and so on—really does pale into insignificance by comparison.

So pause for a moment to think: what is your real main ambition for your child or children? To help you answer that, consider: What was the last reason for which you nagged them? What was the last commitment you arranged for them? What was the last story of frustration you told about them to a friend? I ask these questions not to make you feel guilty. I ask them to help you lift your eyes out of the mud and mess around your feet and look up to the sky, to the stars, to the mountains, to the [insert favourite view here]. Any parent who ponders these things for more than ten seconds will want to give their child a great big hug, pray for them through tears of emotion, and show them Christ in all his beauty. Don't feel guilty. Keep going. Keep your eyes on the prize.

ADOPTED CHILDREN OF GOD

Back to Zacchaeus. He was up a tree. Down the tree. Eating with Jesus. He was lost. He is saved. And so, Jesus says, he is now "a son of Abraham" (Luke 19:9). Abraham was the great forefather of God's people, and Jesus spent a few arguments with the Pharisees showing that membership of Abraham's family was by sharing his faith in God and not his genetic code (see John 8:39-41, 54-59). Zacchaeus, in the only sense that really matters, had placed himself outside Abraham's family through his sin. So had every other citizen of Jericho, wherever they would have placed themselves on the line from "good" to "bad", because God had told his people the standard: "Be holy, because I, the LORD your God, am holy" (Leviticus 19:2). The most well-behaved kid, the most morally upstanding adult, is not *that* holy.

But now here is Zacchaeus, eating with God's Son. Here he is, a son of Abraham. A child in God's own family. That day he became a precious child of the living God, Jesus' own brother, part of an eternal family, never to be let go. He was adopted. He, like every other follower of Jesus who's ever lived, could say:

See what great love the Father has lavished on us, that we should be called children of God! And that is what we are! (1 John 3:1)

We have been adopted! We used to be without a spiritual family. We were alone. Now we have had love poured over us until we are soaked in it. And our new identity has been announced, with a party in heaven. Trumpets. Confetti cannons. Big cakes. Loud music. We are children of God!

My colleague Amy and her husband adopted four children. To make it legally official, they had to go to a court of law. The judge was wonderful. He wanted to make sure that this was a memory the children would hold tight to. He allowed them to wear his judge's wig, bang his hammer, climb over the wooden panelled furniture and take selfies with him. He gave them a certificate. He did all he could to make clear that their lives were now different. Before, they had been in need of parents to care for them. Now, they were Smiths. And that would never change. The judge knew that in the days ahead there would be insecurities to battle, nightmares to navigate, difficult conversations to have, and perhaps years of processing past trauma. But they would work through all that as adopted, beloved children. And that was entirely unaffected by how those children had behaved on the way to the court or how they would behave on the way to their new home afterwards. They were Smiths. That was all that mattered. In honesty, nearly ten years later, after a huge amount of water has gone under the bridge, it is still all that matters. Adoption is another brilliant Bible picture of our identity.

It takes a lifetime to work through what it means to be a Christian. There are daily mistakes. There is daily repentance, daily forgiveness, and daily bread given by God to get through one more day. Our children do not need to leave home with it all worked out. And incidentally, we need to make clear to them that we don't have it all worked out. As parents we need to model that we are a work in progress—we need to let them know our doubts and see our struggles and own our failings. Most of all, we need to keep repeating our identity: we are children of God. We are not good. We are not better. We are not religious. We are saved sinners.

Here is the headline for this chapter: Christianity is not about what we do but about who we are. Before I was a Christian, I had one identity. Before I was a Christian, I was dead. Jesus saved me when, aged 11, I said, "Jesus, sorry for my sin; thank you for dying for me; please help me follow you". So I now have a new identity. I am now alive. That is my story. There are lots of other details. My teenage years felt bumpy. If I'm honest, life still feels bumpy. I am doing my best to show my children that the labels God gives them are the only ones that matter. It feels bumpy. And that is all right.

"See what great love the Father has lavished on us, that we should be called children of God! And that is what we are!" I love an exclamation mark in the Bible. We get two here. I imagine John punching the air as he wrote that second one. He needed to go for a walk after that sentence, to recover his composure. I'm English, so I struggle to display my emotions (or even feel them in the first place). I have a friend who posts videos on social media of what church services look like in Uganda. They would get excited about these exclamation marks. They would dance. For a long time. I want more of Ugandan Christianity in my life! This is the truth about me, and about you, and our greatest aim and highest ambition for our kids must not be that they be well-behaved, well-liked or well-educated, but that, by faith in Jesus, they be children of God.

OH, AND ABOUT BEHAVING...

All parents want children who do the right thing. That is good and right. Identity matters the most, but being good is a thing worth caring about. And the fact is that if we want children to do the right thing, then the best way to go about it is to show them Jesus.

The day that Zacchaeus met Jesus and was saved—the day his identity changed—he also made a monumental change in his behaviour:

> But Zacchaeus stood up and said to the Lord, "Look, Lord! Here and now I give half of my possessions to the poor, and if I have cheated anybody out of anything, I will pay back four times the amount." (Luke 19:8)

Zacchaeus had cheated so many people that paying them all back four times the amount must have left him with very few pennies to rub together. But I don't think he spent long doing the calculations. He had been given a new heart. How much money he had left in the bank was no longer a concern (even though, before that day, it must have been one of the few things he cared about). Those things that he had held closest he now gave away freely.

I worked with children at my last church for twelve years. I ran after-school clubs and Friday-evening socials; I led Sunday School and taught classes. I am in no doubt who the naughtiest boy I ever met was. He was the only boy who ever made me lose my temper. I think I understood some of the underlying reasons for his behaviour; his Dad had made poor decisions which left his son feeling insecure. He had few friends at school, and his methods for making new friends always backfired. The story of Zacchaeus reminds me that for all of those issues—for his bad behaviour, for his defiance, for his insecurity and for his sadness—he needed Jesus. He needed a lot of things, but he needed Jesus most. And none of those things needed to keep that boy from him.

As parents we are the world experts on our children. We are the best placed to make a list of their needs. We know every insecurity. We can (mostly) predict when their behaviour will explode. We know the smallest indicator of their mood. We weep with them. We laugh with them. And we do it all without trying. Join with me in wanting our children to know Jesus before all else. He knows all that they need, and he will get to it (in his own way), but first he wants to adopt them into his family. And if they already are in his family, be patient. The change in their behaviour and decision-making may not be as quick as it was for Zacchaeus, but the Lord is up to something good in their lives.

I'm looking forward to meeting Zacchaeus in the new creation. I think I will still be tall and he will still be short. We will probably need to sit down to talk. I am certain that neither of us will talk about our height, though. We will have things to chat through that matter far more. After all, he's my brother.

Questions to think about...

1. What aspect of your Christian identity do you enjoy the most right now (for instance, "alive" or "child of God" or "healed")?

2. If you're honest, how do you think about Christianity? What are the wrong defining labels you are tempted to give to Christians/yourself/Christianity?

3. Can you see in yourself the desires, ambitions and priorities you have for your child? Which are deliberate? Which are you pleased to hold? Which are your children aware of?

4. What identity labels do you think your child would own for themselves, Christian or otherwise?

3

I AM PRECIOUS TO GOD

I was walking along a beach when I saw a small girl crying. She was standing alone with her toes in the lapping sea, totally still, looking up the beach with tears rolling down her cheeks. I guessed she was three years old. She was clearly lost, and she clearly wanted a parent. She couldn't see anyone she knew on the crowded beach. I stopped next to her. I looked around. I couldn't see anyone calling to her or walking to pick her up. I crouched down next to her to talk to her. Then her big brother appeared next to her. She looked relieved. I probably did too. He took her hand and dragged her through the crowds towards a slightly embarrassed parent.

That's just one example of a truth so old that we hardly need to say it out loud: children need parents. In a moment of fear, a child runs to their parent. In the arms of a loving parent, a child's situation is transformed. Insecurity becomes security. It is one of the most basic building blocks of society—a child needs the loving care of at least one parent. It's why fostering and adoption are necessary and wonderful. Children who have had secure, loving relationships are more likely to flourish in life.

PRECIOUS?

Knowing we are precious to another is the foundation of who we are.

Does that suddenly make you feel a little insecure? *How precious am I? How much care have I received? How many people love me?*

My friend Rachel remembers her childhood house being broken into. She came home from school to find the police at her home while her parents searched for what had been stolen. Her mum held up her empty Mickey Mouse moneybox with a sad apology. Rachel didn't care. She ran past her mum and into her bedroom, heart pounding in fear. What if they had taken her most prized possession? Relief! There she was, slumped over on her pillow—Rachel's most treasured possession: Georgie Girl. She picked up her tattered chimpanzee (to clarify, Georgie Girl was a stuffed toy, not a real chimpanzee!). She checked back and front. Unharmed! What idiots those burglars were to have left her. What a good job that they were distracted by the moneybox and therefore missed the truly priceless item in the room.

Value is announced and decided by another. Rachel said Georgie was precious to her, so she was. I say my child is precious to me, and it does not matter to me if every single other human in the world announces, with one voice, that my child is not precious—they still are. Because I say so. Enough said.

The problem for our children is that it is very easy for them (as it is for their parents) to listen to the wrong *another*. Even those from the most secure, loving homes suddenly feel shaken over the smallest issue. They are left insecure by things that may sound trivial to us but are so, so important to them:

- No one sat with me at lunch.
- I didn't get an invitation to her party.
- I need a pair of *those* trainers.
- I'm never picked for a sports team.
- I am the only one without an iPhone.
- They called me ugly.
- I hate always being alone.

This might also be the moment to admit that our reasons, as parents, for feeling insecure are not that different— they're just grown-up versions of the same things:

- I feel left out of a social group among the school parents or in my church.
- I don't have the right clothes.
- I missed out on the promotion at work.
- I can't do home improvement like others can.
- Someone, either today or years ago, commented negatively about my appearance, and I can't shake it.
- I hate being alone.

As parents, we frequently don't feel secure. We don't feel precious enough.

Our kids need to know that we love them—that they are precious to us. When they're three, knowing just that is basically enough. There's safety and security in our arms and, knowing that, they can (most of the time) face the world at toddler group and in Sunday school. By the time they're 13, our children still need to know that we love them and they're precious to us—they may even want to experience safety and security in our arms—but that's not enough. That's hard for us, but it's understandable—after all, it's not enough for you to know that your parents think you're amazing.

Our children do need a loving parent, or two loving parents. But they need more than that to know they are precious. They need *another* who is bigger and better than you and me.

And that is what they have.

GOD SAYS YOU'RE PRECIOUS

God planned to make you. Then God did make you. And now God says you are the best thing he has made (along with a few others!). God says you are precious. His opinion won't change on that. Anyone who makes you feel anything other than priceless needs to take it up with him (but if you are kind, you won't recommend that they do):

> God said, "Let us make mankind in our image, in our likeness, so that they may rule over the fish in the sea and the birds in the sky, over the livestock and all the wild

animals, and over all the creatures that move along the ground." (Genesis 1:26)

Nothing ever just happens. God made a decision. Without that decision you wouldn't be here. Nothing else in all of creation is made in his likeness—only people. We are like him. So we are more precious than anything else. Every human is precious in God's sight.

> So God created mankind in his own image,
> in the image of God he created them;
> male and female he created them. (v 27)

What God plans, God does. He made people. Deliberately. In a beautiful way, made like himself. So we really *are* valuable.

> God saw all that he had made, and it was **very** good.
> (v 31, emphasis added)

It makes me smile that the dolphins, turtles, gurgling streams, stars and oak trees (to name a few of my favourite things—I prefer my list to Julie Andrews') got a "good" from God, but when he looked upon man and woman, God said, "Very good". That is the verdict that echoes through time into your heart. His verdict on us (and our children) is not dependent on our feelings, our achievements, our salary, our goodness, or the opinion of others. You can say with certainty, "I am made by God. I am precious to God." Even if everyone else, with one voice, were to say to you, "You are worth very little", God still stands by you and says, *I made you a little like myself. So you are precious. I say so. Enough said.*

In the end, then, the question is which "another" will we listen to when it comes to our sense of self-worth and security—God, or someone else?

And which will we encourage and lead our kids to listen to?

When your child doubts their value, imagine the conversation they are having with God: *You invented me and made me a little like you. You announced to the watching world that you made me very good. You are the all-knowing, all-powerful, supreme eternal being. You say I am precious. I hear that. But I'm standing here feeling worthless because...*

- *I find reading hard.*

- *my trainers don't have a swoosh on the side.*

- *Billy says I have no friends / am weird / am too short / am a loser [delete as applicable].*

- *this arbitrary boy has not yet announced that I am more beautiful than [insert current airbrushed fashionable social influencer here].*

Of course, we're not in Eden anymore. Genesis 3 happened, when the first humans, even as the words "very good" were echoing around their perfect garden, decided to reject God and seek their sense of security and worth elsewhere. We live in a fallen world, which means that every single moment, person and situation is tainted by sin. Everything is at least a little broken, and a fair proportion is a total mess. So we frequently don't feel "very good", and when we do, it is often for all the wrong reasons, achieved at the expense of others or due to a fairly arbitrary achievement on our part. There is much about us that is not "very good". Yet, despite that, it remains God's settled, clear decision that we are "very good", because he created us precious. No sin, whether it's ours or someone else's, can extinguish our made-in-God's-image-ness. We may be broken mirrors, but we're mirrors nonetheless.

WHAT STUFFED TOYS TEACH US ABOUT GOD

I have a long history of being late. For everything. (Except once, when I was exactly a month early for a meeting.) We were once late leaving for a ferry. We had driven for about 15 minutes when my wife asked where Robot, the stuffed android toy and most-valued possession of one of my children, was. It is the question I fear. As I drove, the rest of the family searched for Robot. There was no Robot. There was a silence. Everyone was looking at me. Would Dad drive back for Robot? I weighed up my options. Miss the ferry or discover the impact on my holiday due to a missing stuffed android? We went back. Got Robot. Then left. Again. I did not say a word for the two-hour journey to the (missed) ferry. That is a lot of anger. (I did apologise to my family for my anger as we boarded the later ferry.)

Each of my children has had a stuffed toy that they could not be without. (If you are in that phase of life, let me assure you that your child will not take their stuffed toy to their first job interview. They do grow out of it.) My children would have done *anything* to rescue those favourite toys. Each of those toys had flaws, and more as they aged and became threadbare. But each child would never have swapped their toy for a newer one, a cleaner one or a bigger one. They are precious beyond measure.

Can we convince our children that God holds us as precious beyond measure in the same way that they see their favourite stuffed toy? He made us. He knows our sins and our flaws. (And as parents, we feel like our flaws increase as we age, and we experience becoming more threadbare.) Yet still, we are precious to the Creator of everything. And he has not only *said* we are precious to him; he has *shown* us. His decision to rescue us was far more costly than a missed ferry. It took Jesus, the divine second Person of the Trinity, to the cross. We see how precious we are to our Creator at the cross. He never forgot that he had made us *very good*.

This can make all the difference to you as a parent, and to your kids.

If your child is the only one of their age who can't yet speak or read or spell, you can still be certain that they are precious to the one who spoke planets into place. Their own words (or lack of them) will never determine their value because his words already have.

If your child is the only one in their class not to be invited to a party, you can explain why God's care for them matters far more. He made them, and he wants to spend time with them, so he made sure that they were invited to his forever party. Whose invitation would they rather receive?

If your child's faith marks them out for persecution of some kind (as it inevitably will), of course they will wish that they could belong to the crowd rather than be the outsider. You can explain to them that they can prize their Creator's delight, so that they need not worry so much about that of their teacher or their peer group.

And in those moments when your child is not being particularly loveable (and let's be honest, there are those moments) and you are struggling to love them, you can pause and thank the Lord that, in spite of your own flaws and lack of loveliness, in *every* moment he holds you precious—and holds your kids equally precious too. And then you can tell them about his unwavering love even as you admit the weaknesses of your own.

SO LISTEN

I smile when I hear my children whisper into the ear of our dog. They tell him of their love. They tell him jokes. They tell him which part of his body is their favourite. They look into his eyes and make incredible promises to him. I wonder what he is thinking. (I know that he is probably thinking about dog food and the smell of other dogs' bottoms, but it doesn't stop me wondering.) Our dog needs to know the voice of my children. He needs to listen to them. I pity the dog owner whose dog does not return to them when *called*. It is a pitiful sight. Picture the dog owner whose dog never responds to their voice.

Picture the created person who never responds to the voice of their Creator.

If our children understand how precious they are to their Creator, then they will know that it is good to listen to him. This is the foundation of our faith. We were made very good by him and we are precious to him, so we choose to listen carefully:

- We will continue going to church even if we struggle to focus. We gather to listen together.

- We will keep opening the Bible as a family together, when we can, because it is who we are. We are a family of listeners.

- We will talk about God's care and his ways, with each other, with friends and with strangers, even when we don't physically open a Bible, even if it feels awkward. We want others to listen.

- We will talk in our families about the Spirit's work in our lives and pray for his help when it's all gone wrong—when we've snapped, screamed, shouted, or done things we are ashamed of—because he is our Creator, and none of this surprises him, and he still chooses to love us. We listen when we'd prefer to hide.

LOVE AND AUTHORITY

"Why should I?" is never what I want to hear from my children. It is them testing the boundaries. It can come with a touch of snarl, just after I have asked them to do something. In that moment of raw confrontation, it is tempting to bark back, "Because I said so!" We find a better answer in one of the most famous "parenting passages":

Children, obey your parents in the Lord, for this is right. "Honour your father and mother"—which is the first commandment with a promise—"so that it may go well with you and that you may enjoy long life on the earth." Fathers, do not exasperate your children; instead, bring them up in the training and instruction of the Lord.
(Ephesians 6:1-4)

As parents, we may want to focus here on "Children, obey your parents" because it gives us a free pass to make any and every demand on our children. Instead, it is the "in the Lord" that needs to catch our attention. Children here are asked to obey their parents as if they are obeying Christ. There is something more happening here than just simply *Listen to your parent because they're the boss.* God has placed parents in the life of his created image bearers for them to learn how to relate to him. Parents are placed between our children and God, just for a season, to teach them this beautiful loving, trusting relationship. What a responsibility, to be the shadow of God in their lives!

As Jesus called God "*Abba,* Father" (*Abba* meaning something like "Dad" in his Aramaic mother tongue), in Christ, as God's adopted children, we get to also call him "*Abba,* Father" (Mark 14:36; Romans 8:15). As Christian parents, we learn to call God our true, better Dad, obeying him above all others as he loves us more than all others love us.

Our task is to teach this to our children. As they learn that our love is a strong love that they can depend on, they will discover from us that it is a shadow of their heavenly Father's love. If we do our job properly, our children will learn to obey us because we will be modelling the steadfast love that God offers them. If they can trust us to be acting for their good (even when they disagree) in the everyday, then we are teaching them to trust that their better heavenly Father is even more worthy of their obedience. As we bring them up "in the training and instruction of the Lord", we are encouraging and equipping them to know God as their Father for themselves, without our influence or us showing them.

Children who obey their godly parents in this way are given an astonishing promise—a long life! That takes us by surprise. We might be used to the idea that we receive spiritual blessings in Christ, where we are promised unseen heavenly riches, every imaginable spiritual blessing and future eternal life (see Ephesians 1:3; 1 Peter 1:3-4). But here our children are promised the physical, visible blessing now of a long life. Before we scoff, mutter and nitpick at this plain meaning, wonder with me at what government policy could be rolled out that would do more to improve the lives of children than godly parents showing their child the Lord as their Creator, telling them of their inalienable worth as his precious image-bearers, and seeking to encourage them to live a godly life while under their parental responsibility. How much money would a government need to spend on education, social services and health to bring about the same results?

It is a blessing beyond measure for children to have parents who seek to show them that as created image-bearers, they are loved by God and should therefore listen to God—both because it is right and because it is the way most likely to lead to a long, flourishing life. Aim to be, and pray you'll be, the kind of parent who shows how good it is to be loved by God and how good it is to be under his loving authority.

Questions to think about...

1. Being totally honest, how would you complete this sentence: "I am valuable because..."?

2. Can you spot clues to where your child finds their sense of value? What are the circumstances in which they struggle to feel valuable? When do they feel priceless?

3. Can you think of a recent moment when your family needed to hear God say, *I made you a little like myself. So you are precious. I say so. Enough said*? In what probable future family moment would you like to remember to share this truth?

4

I AM FORGIVEN

Parenting involves repeating yourself over and over again.

When I was growing up, some of those repetitions became family catchphrases. When trying on new clothes, I would look at myself from every angle in the mirror. (To this day, I have no real clue what I am meant to be looking for.) After an age, my mum would ask, "But do you feel comfortable? Because if you don't feel comfortable in it, you will never wear it." She wasn't just talking about the fit—it was a deeper question for my teenage self to ponder. Was this clothing me? Did I want to look like this? Being a functional kind of guy, I would answer the question by putting the colourful patterns back on the rail and asking mum to pay for the bland option.

This generation of children are encouraged to do what feels comfortable to them. And the choices now go far deeper than clothes. Be true to yourself. Follow your heart. Be who you want to be. Find your gift. Search out your passion. Don't let anyone stand in the way. Beat your own path. Ignore convention.

A modern mantra for the younger generation is "You do you". It tells each person to look deep inside themselves to find out who they are and then to be that person, whatever anyone else says or whatever doubts they may have. That is always the Western world's answer to guilt, disappointment and emptiness. Sin is no longer the worst thing you can do—now, it's to not be true to yourself.

But what if our hearts are the problem, because our hearts are always chasing after the next big thing? *I need the new football boots. I have to be the star of the show. I will do anything for more friends. I must win this match. I need to come first in my class.* What if our hearts lead us away from who we were made to be instead of towards it? What if being true to ourselves ends up hurting those who get in their way? What if beating your own path leads to a less, not more, comfortable place?

The "gospel" of the Western world tells our kids that their biggest problem is not following their desires; that their biggest failure would be not following their heart or fulfilling their potential, or preventing someone else from following theirs; and that they will find freedom by ignoring any sense of guilt and find themselves by looking within.

The Christian gospel is therefore going to sound odd. Your kids' biggest problem is following their sinful desires, and their biggest failure is not to admit their wrongdoing and return to God; they will only find freedom by acknowledging their guilt and asking for forgiveness; and they will find themselves by returning home to God and letting him run things.

One of those gospels has no answers for when our kids don't live up to the dream of being the person they want to be, or when circumstances prevent them achieving their potential, or when they can't pursue their goals, or when they just meet deep disappointment in life. The other offers the freedom to be honest, and it offers forgiveness, acceptance and a fresh start.

Our task is to root our kids in the gospel that is not only true but better. And that means our kids need to have a sense that they are sinners, but they also need to know that grace is always available, always triumphs, and always brings a joy that cannot be found anywhere else. Our kids need to know that the greatest story in the world is to be able to say, "I once was lost, but now I'm found."

EVERY PARENT'S NIGHTMARE

The beginning of the story Jesus tells about the "prodigal son" will be familiar to most of us:

> *There was a man who had two sons. The younger one said to his father, "Father, give me my share of the estate." So he divided his property between them.*
>
> *Not long after that, the younger son got together all he had [and] set off for a distant country. (Luke 15:11-13)*

We tend to read the story standing in the shoes of the younger son, rather than the father (which is right: the father represents God, and we're not God). But for a moment, read those lines *as a parent*. I feel something in the pit of my stomach. While our children are young, they live at home with us and spend several years rarely more than a few yards from us. There are times when we wonder if there will ever be a day when we can take a shower without them being in the room with us. Does any parent imagine that a day will come when their child leaves home and does not get in touch again for *years*? That's not a part of the parenting journey that any of us have planned for.

Yet here is exactly that moment in this father's life. It chills my heart to imagine my son, on the edge of adulthood, saying to me, "Dad, it's time for me to go. I have waited long enough. I can't wait any longer for you to die. I want every good thing you have, and, to be honest, I don't want you in my life. Don't visit or contact me. I want to live my best life, and I don't know where that will be, but I know it won't be here with you. I'll be leaving tomorrow."

If it was a business transaction, it might make some sense—a transfer of wealth from one generation to the next, to be invested for growth. But this is a family being broken apart with a conversation where only the son speaks. The son has done the thinking. He has looked down the years and made some decisions. He is clear that his life will be better *with* his dad's money and *without* his dad.

AT HOME

Even now that I'm middle-aged, I still love visiting my parents. (I know this is not something everyone can say, often for justifiable and painful reasons.) I love the way my dad comes out of their home before I can get to the doorbell. I am tall, but my dad is taller, and so his arms still wrap around me and squeeze. Dad puts me in a chair in the kitchen and offers me a drink. He wants me to rest. He cares. My heart feels at peace and at home.

In that moment, I'm glimpsing what the Bible calls *shalom*: feeling at peace and at home. It's what the prophets talked about as the Spirit enabled them to gaze into the future, past the sin and mess and brokenness of the world they knew, and we still know:

> *The wolf will live with the lamb, the leopard will lie down with the goat, the calf and the lion and the yearling together; and a little child will lead them. (Isaiah 11:6)*

> *My people will live in peaceful dwelling-places, in secure homes, in undisturbed places of rest. (32:18)*

> *They will not labour in vain, nor will they bear children doomed to misfortune; for they will be a people blessed by the* LORD, *they and their descendants with them. (65:23)*

This will be our story when Christ returns and puts all things right. The rest, joy and beauty I crave *will* come. I want this for my whole family. I ache to be in that place with them. When I think about Isaiah's description, I see the huge difference between the new creation and the very best of our life as a family now. This place that Isaiah promises cannot be my family's story yet—but, if we all keep trusting Christ, one day it will be. It's shalom: a word for which the translation "peace" is too limited. Shalom is belonging in the heart of a loving family. It is unruffled relationships. It is settled delight. It is beauty and deep breaths. It is safety and trust. It is how things ought to be. It is being home with our Father and never having to leave.

And in Jesus' parable, it is shalom that the son decides to step out of. He wants to escape from shalom. He wants to be as far away from shalom as possible. This is sin— breaking shalom. And it is stupid. Who would run away from shalom? Answer: an idiot.

We need to be clear on what sin is, and we need to help our kids be clear too.

Jesus' parable helps us see that the Christian concept of sin is not about naughty behaviour or even a wrong lifestyle— it is about an attitude towards God, the one who loves us most. It is about identity. It is deep within us. It is the instinct of our hearts to fill our pockets with God's good gifts of health, laughter, wealth, relationships, nature and so on, and to walk away from him. Sin does not start with a list of wrong things done; it starts with a broken relationship with our Creator. At its heart, sin is breaking that shalom that God offers. Because he is our loving Creator, he knows exactly how to give us shalom. The problem is, we tell him we know better. We are the goldfish that throws itself out of its fishbowl in order to be free.

It is helpful for a parent to understand and remember the difference: sin is a heart issue, not a behaviour issue. If we understand this, then when our kids break a rule, we will seek to see beyond the wrong behaviour to the heart-cause. That will take us to a deeper issue and to a different solution—to their need for forgiveness rather than their need to moderate their behaviour. (More on this in the next chapter.)

Side note: We want shalom for our children, and so we need to aim for our homes to be places where shalom is glimpsed. We want our kids to enjoy belonging, safety, security and certainty in their family under God's loving care. This is why our homes should have rules: we don't allow unkind words to be said to each other (because it divides the loving unity); we don't allow talking back to parents (because it rips apart the good order God has given); we insist on coming to church together (because we want to enjoy fellowship and worship together). These are rules of a different kind to those that simply safeguard our own selfish preferences ("No talking during the big football game").

THE YOUNGER SON COMES BACK

Not long after that, the younger son got together all he had, set off for a distant country and there squandered his wealth in wild living. After he had spent everything, there was a severe famine in that whole country, and he began to be in need. So he went and hired himself out to a citizen of that country, who sent him to his fields to feed pigs. He longed to fill his stomach with the pods that the pigs were eating, but no one gave him anything.

(Luke 15:13-16)

Before long, the younger son realised that the belonging that the world offers comes at a price—everything he has.

The friends he bought with money disappear when it's gone, and he's left alone. In his pigsty moment, when he can stoop no lower, he remembers what true belonging felt like and where he enjoyed it: at home with his father. He heads home, head bowed, speech rehearsed... and flying towards him comes love—the father's embrace.

> *But while he was still a long way off, his father saw him and was filled with compassion for him; he ran to his son, threw his arms round him and kissed him.*
>
> *The son said to him, "Father, I have sinned against heaven and against you. I am no longer worthy to be called your son."*
>
> *But the father said to his servants, "Quick! Bring the best robe and put it on him. Put a ring on his finger and sandals on his feet. Bring the fattened calf and kill it. Let's have a feast and celebrate. For this son of mine was dead and is alive again; he was lost and is found." So they began to celebrate. (v 20-24)*

The prodigal son is home like he's never been home before, because this time he knows there is nowhere else he'd rather be.

The father is the hero of the story. He is the one who runs, who hugs, who interrupts and who throws the party. He is the one who changes the identity of the younger son from lost to found.

It is wonderful how this one story covers so much of what we and our children need to understand. The son is held responsible for his actions. He got it wrong. He had no excuses and did not offer any. It is not, as we often hear it, that all our wrong decisions can be traced back to our upbringing or our environment. The son is no victim. He is responsible. He got it wrong. But the father never stopped looking. His love is vast. His forgiveness is total. This is the father we hold out to our children: the God of grace.

I was once on a panel that was aiming to help parents think these things through. We were taking questions. One dad asked, "How do we show grace in our homes?" I was feeling smug. I knew the answer! "We forgive freely." He came back: "But should I surprise my daughter by tidying her room, after I have told her ten times to do it? Should I lower my expectations of her behaviour? Should I have no rules?" I have thought about his question so much since that evening. How do we show grace without throwing out all discipline, all authority and all wisdom?

The father in the parable helps us to answer that question. Grace is in the air of that father's home. It is everywhere. It's in the run; it's in the hug; it's in the party. And at no point does it feel like the father is wondering quietly to himself, *But maybe he'll do it again if I show him this much grace...?* This is what God is like. Our Father is a flood of grace.

As parents we do need to set boundaries, hold our children responsible for their actions, and discipline them fairly and calmly, as our heavenly Father disciplines us (Hebrews 12:10-11). There should be warnings and consequences in our homes for our children's bad behaviour. As God has been clear with us in the Bible on the behaviours he expects of us, so we need to be clear and consistent with our children. And as with our heavenly Father, we need to be acting out of love (rather than frustration or selfish anger) throughout, waiting for and aiming for the hug, for the homecoming. We are to seek to be like God in how we show grace to our children. But more than that, we are to try to show them that God's grace is far greater than ours. There is nothing they could do that cannot be forgiven by our heavenly Father.

Are we ready as parents to be full of grace on the day when our children come back from an addiction, from sexual sin or from choices that damaged our lives? The choice at the pigsty is hard, but it is made easier if you know that your heavenly Father will run towards you, rather than turn away from you. And it is far easier to know this if you have experienced the safe and certain knowledge that your earthly parents are like that—that grace is in the air of your parental home.

The younger son needed to learn that he could come back home. The other son needs to learn how he belongs there.

THE OLDER SON CLEARS OUT

There is, famously, a second brother in the story—the older one, who has worked hard and stayed with his dad, and believes he's earned his place in the home on the basis of his behaviour. So when his sinful brother returns, he's outraged by the treatment the father gives him. *Where's my party?* he demands:

Look! All these years I've been slaving for you and never disobeyed your orders. Yet you never gave me even a young goat so I could celebrate with my friends. But when this son of yours who has squandered your property with prostitutes comes home, you kill the fattened calf for him!

(Luke 15:29-30)

He thought he'd missed out by staying home with his father. He'd obeyed like a servant and expected celebration for his efforts. He had never strayed far from his father, and yet still he didn't know who he himself was—a dearly loved son who was loved beyond measure. Because he'd approached life with a transactional rather than a relational attitude, he'd never enjoyed the shalom that was all around him. He'd grimly got on with his work so that his father would have to bless him, rather than enjoying the father who wanted to bless him.

Some children are like the younger son. They're easy to spot. Their parents have their heads in their hands. Their teacher has to speak to their parents regularly. These children expect long conversations about their behaviour. They *know* they are getting it wrong.

Some children are like the older son. They're harder to spot. They behave well. Their teachers are only ever pleased. They sit nicely. They receive praise. They expect praise. But their hearts are hard. They might know all the right answers in Sunday school but they don't feel the delight of serving their God. Their obedience is to earn praise, not obeying out of a thankful heart.

Jesus fully understands the hearts of both sons, and he shares his Father's heart. Whether your child rebels and runs away or stays at home trying to be good and earn love,

Jesus told this story to bring both to their senses. He lived, died and rose again to take the sins of the selfish rebellion of younger brothers *and* of the selfish pride of older ones. Whichever son your child is, they need to know two things: first, that their hearts are sinful; and second and supremely, that as they see the truth of this, they can always run home to their Father's embrace and know forgiveness and a love they could never earn and can never lose—the love of a Father with whom they completely belong.

THE CHILD WHO ISN'T IN THE STORY

There is one type of child who is not featured in Jesus' parable—the child we pray our kids will prove to be.

This a parable, the last in a set of three that Jesus uses to teach two sets of people:

> *The tax collectors and sinners were all gathering round to hear Jesus. But the Pharisees and the teachers of the law muttered, "This man welcomes sinners, and eats with them." (v 1-2)*

He's speaking to those who feel furthest from God (in "the tax collectors and sinners") and to those who *wrongly* believe they are close to God ("the Pharisees and the teachers of the law"). Those two categories do not describe every single person. The soft-hearted disciple is not in this parable.

I remember how I learned that not all kids are younger or older brothers. I was teaching the account of creation to the children of my church. I ran through the six days of creation. I reached the seventh day. I said that God took a rest—that he took it easy. I used a visual on the screen of a bed to represent that rest. A hand went up. Little Becky said, "God doesn't sleep". I felt put out; a small child was telling me off and spoiling my point. Afterwards I was speaking to her parents and mentioned her comment to them. Becky's dad replied, "Ah, she'll have said that because she is scared of the dark. She needs to know that she can sleep peacefully because God doesn't. He is awake and with her, in the dark." I had been corrected—not so much by that dad but by the Spirit. I had taken Becky as an "older son", proud to know the right answer and taking the opportunity to look clever. In fact, she was speaking from a soft-hearted place of reliance on God as her Father, who does not sleep and who watched over her all night.

The soft-hearted child disciple is not a myth. We do not have to assume—in fact, we should not assume—that all kids are younger brothers or older brothers. We can pray that our kids will simply be children of their heavenly Father, enjoying his love, his forgiveness, his presence and his care. And, if we see the Spirit growing that kind of heart in our kids, we can give huge thanks.

A PLACE OF GRACE

A friend's teenage daughter struggles with planning, concentration and holding multiple instructions in her mind for any length of time. This makes school difficult. She's conscientious and wants to fit in, so she (mostly) manages not to express the anxiety and frustration that she's feeling in the classroom. But she comes home like a coiled spring after a day of being on edge and desperately holding it all together. When she gets to the safety of her family, suddenly the spring is released and her behaviour is, well, sub-optimal! Before her mum recognised her difficulties, they often found themselves stuck in a cycle of frustration and disappointment. Now, her mum can better speak into her world. The behaviour isn't excused but now it is understood, and they're learning to deal with it together more constructively.

A deeper understanding of our children will not excuse what is wrong and sinful in their lives, but it does help us to understand why our children struggle in particular ways. Knowing our kids means we can then respond with compassion. Grace does not mean we ignore the sin, but it does mean we wrap our child in robes of forgiveness— ours and Christ's. Grace welcomes home—grace says, "You belong here and you're loved here".

Our families are where our kids' true hearts are exposed. The last biscuit, the shove, the discouraging word, the accidental bump on the stairs, the selfish complaint. These moments are not simply irritations that disrupt my life (though they do). These are opportunities when God is calling us to something bigger than our own comfort. These are the moments when God calls us to love our children and not give in to the quick (shouted, angry, impatient) solutions but rather to address the sin as sin and to point them towards restoration and forgiveness and a fresh start.

Our families reveal our own hearts too. Most of us didn't know how much we struggled with impatience until we became parents. We may even discover through our parenting whether we are naturally the younger son or the older son. Are we wanting to push our children away, to be free, to be independent, to be selfish? Or are we diligently doing everything to serve our children, but beneath lies the seething, bitter heart of the martyr? We belong at home with the father, just like our children. His grace is sufficient even for us.

I started with one of my Mum's catchphrases: "But do you feel comfortable?" I know that now I have my own parental catchphrases. Years from now, my children will (hopefully) laugh about the things I kept saying, just as I laugh with my siblings about our parents' repeated mantras.

What is the catchphrase you would choose for your child to remember? What would you like to say so often that your child interrupts to finish it for you? Let it be something that is full of grace.

Questions to think about...

1. Can you see the heart of the younger son or the older son in yourself? In your children?

2. Have you ever seen a moment of soft-hearted reliance on God in your family? Pray for it. Look for it. Highlight it. Thank God for it.

3. For what grace that you see in your family can you pause and thank God for right now? (If you are a Christian, I know there will be something!)

5

I CAN CHANGE

I'm going to assume just for a moment that your kids are much like mine: that is, not perfect. And I'm going to assume, therefore, that right now you can name a few ways that you have told your kids, over the past few days, to be different, to behave better, to change.

This chapter is focussing on behaviour. But really, it's actually about the heart.

I remember sitting in a doctor's waiting room hearing a Mum saying, "Share!" over and over again to her children. Each time she grew a little louder. After the eighth time, I wanted to shout equally loudly, "Stop shouting, 'Share!' at your children!" (I didn't.)

If a parent shouts, "Share!" at their children loudly and often enough, they probably will share—eventually. Why? To stop their parent shouting at them. Have they learnt to share? No. Are they more likely to share next time? Yes, if their parents are in the room (because they don't want to be shouted at). No, if their parents are not (because sharing means they lose out).

A few years ago, we got our first family dog. I discovered that you have to train a puppy to do *everything*. Children are quite like puppies. With a constant process of repetition and reward, we can train a child to be broadly civilised. Wearing shoes, brushing teeth and washing hands after going to the loo can be imposed on our children by constant nagging (or "training"). But we want more for our children than that.

If we could train them out of sin through routine and habit, then they wouldn't need Jesus Christ to have died for them, and we could write the ultimate parenting book! But we can't. We need Jesus to do a lifelong work in our children for change that lasts.

Jesus told a parable to explain exactly how our children's behaviour can be improved.

> No good tree bears bad fruit, nor does a bad tree bear good fruit. Each tree is recognised by its own fruit. People do not pick figs from thorn-bushes, or grapes from briers. A good man brings good things out of the good stored up in his heart, and an evil man brings evil things out of the evil stored up in his heart. For the mouth speaks what the heart is full of. (Luke 6:43-45)

Apple trees grow apples. Strawberry plants grow strawberries. If you want to get a strawberry from an apple tree, you'd have to tape strawberries to an apple tree. You could then pick strawberries from an apple tree, but it would be ridiculous. This is the level of gardening advice that Jesus is offering here! Why would he spend precious moments of teaching time on reminding his followers not to expect strawberries to grow on an apple tree? Because he is about to teach them something that is so counterintuitive that he starts with an illustration so obvious and simple that no one can argue.[1]

Jesus explained that expecting improved behaviour ("good things") from an unchanged, sinful ("evil") heart is like expecting an apple tree to grow strawberries. To shout (or say) "Share!" repeatedly at a child is like taping strawberries to an apple tree. You might get improved behaviour for a while, but you are choosing an ineffective method that will not produce lasting change.

Instead, Jesus says that just as apples come only from an apple tree, so truly good behaviour comes from a warm, soft heart that is being changed by the work of his Spirit. This is the story of every Christian. We are not the people we once were. The Spirit is doing a slow, steady work in all Christians to make us more like Christ (Galatians 5:16-24). This is why the Bible repeatedly uses the illustration of fruit. Growth is often discouragingly slow, taking years before there is a harvest, but it is *real* growth.

---

1 I am grateful to Paul Tripp for this explanation of this passage in *Instruments in the Redeemer's Hands* (P&R, 2002).

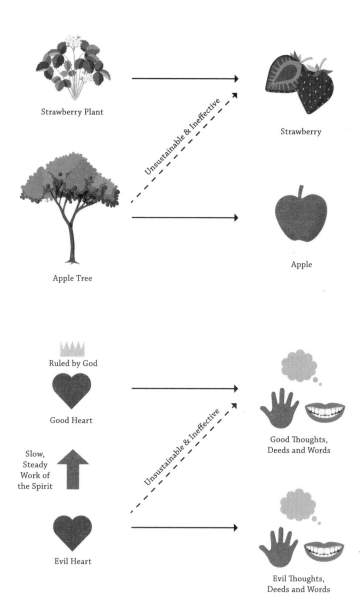

So our parenting needs to focus on the heart, not on the behaviour. This may sound obvious, but it is harder, it is more frustrating, and it requires deliberate effort. We will always tend towards modifying our kids' behaviour rather than helping them think about their heart.

But it's not just their heart under the microscope here. It's ours too.

Perhaps more than in any other aspect of our lives, it is in our parenting where our true motivations and desires are laid bare. Often, I am the one who is most surprised in my parenting. I am learning about myself, and not all of it is good news. I did not know that I had a sharp anger until I became a parent. Nothing else provokes me as my children can. It is not their fault. It is my heart's—that part of me that is the core of me but so often feels like it is not under my control.

Which means that if we're to parent our kids' hearts well, so that they really change, then we're going to need to think about our own hearts too.

TALK ABOUT THE WALK

I have always looked on in awe at families where household chores are done by glorious routine without argument or pleading. Every discussion with one of our children about a chore feels, well... like a chore.

Recently we had one of those moments with my 8-year-old son. The list of chores was growing. The dishwasher needed emptying (and refilling), the lunch table needed laying and the clothes needed hanging up. He refused to do any of the tasks. I told him to do them and explained that the alternative was a full hour in his room.

He preferred to go to his room for the hour (and he timed it himself) rather than do a job.

After the hour had passed, we had a similar exchange of views. He was on his way to the bedroom for another hour when I restrained my stubbornness and anger enough to have a proper conversation (about his stubbornness and anger. I am not blind to the cause!). We sat down together to talk about how someone will make his lunch, someone else will wash his clothes and someone else still will clear away the lunch.

He asked permission to go back to his room for an hour.

I reminded him about the last time he cleaned the bathroom (which he is bizarrely good at). He is good at doing some chores. In that moment, he could choose the chore that he wanted to do.

"Can I go to my bedroom now?" No progress.

I said, "You know, Jesus was the most powerful, important person ever to walk this earth. But he came to earth not to be served but to serve others. He came to die for you. He chose to do the worst, hardest, messiest job we can imagine. We choose to serve one another, rather than waiting to be served by someone else. That is the Christian life."

I watched as I saw the penny drop. He didn't want to go to his bedroom anymore. He was ready to be helpful.

What I noticed was the effect on *my* heart of this process.

I chose not to be angry. I chose not to send him to his bedroom *again*. I chose to remain calm. I chose to take the time. I chose to make this about him learning and growing instead of me winning the confrontation.

Change happens in the heart. Change can happen in his heart. Usually change has to happen in mine too. When change happens in the heart, fruit follows.

To address our children's hearts requires conversations in the home that take place away from the heat of the behavioural crisis, in which we ask good questions, speak gently, and finish with prayer. This is how we bring Jesus Christ into the mess and chaos of everyday life. For most Christian parents, these sorts of conversations don't come naturally. They require practice and effort. But they are worth it, because the Bible says this is how real change happens, and the data backs that up. *Handing Down the Faith* is research based on 215 interviews to discover how parents successfully hand on faith to their children. After analysing all the data, the authors concluded:

> *"If there were only one practical take-away from our research, it would be this: parents need not only to 'walk the walk' but also regularly to talk with their children about their walk, what it means, why it matters, why they care."*[2]

---

2 Christian Smith and Amy Adamczyk, *Handing Down the Faith: How Parents Pass their Religion on to the Next Generation* (Oxford University Press, 2021), p 225.

CHANGE IS INEVITABLE

Where we have got to so far may have left our parenting strategy in the bin:

1. Focusing on improving our children's behaviour alone is as effective in the long term as taping strawberries to an apple tree.

2. If we want to go to work on our children's heart, we will need to go to work on our own heart first.

That feels difficult—impossible, even. In the short term, it's so much more achievable just to snap "Share!" and watch our kids reluctantly obey (eventually). Real change seems out of reach—for us and for our kids. I remember one of my sons mumbling through his tears, "But I can't be good. I can't get it right." We had a great conversation about that—and the focus was not his behaviour or self-control:

We all show the Lord's glory, and we are being changed to be like him. This change in us brings more and more glory. And it comes from the Lord, who is the Spirit.

(2 Corinthians 3:18, ICB)

The truth is, if you are a Christian, you are changing! You are not doomed to repeat your mistakes on an endless loop. You are becoming more like Jesus Christ. That is not an empty mantra. We are changing because the power of the Holy Spirit, the living God himself, is at work in every Christian.

Anyone who is a Christian has the Spirit of God at work in them (Romans 8:9, 14). As we explain this to our children, there is an inevitable question: "How do I know

I have the Spirit? I don't feel any different." You can ask them two questions to help them answer their question (and if they don't understand the questions, what a great opportunity!):

1. Do you believe that Jesus died for you so that you could be forgiven for everything?

2. Do you pray to God as your Father in heaven, trusting him to hear you?

If a child can say yes to both, then they can be confident that they have the Spirit...

And if the Spirit of him who raised Jesus from the dead is living in you, he who raised Christ from the dead will also give life to your mortal bodies because of his Spirit who lives in you. (Romans 8:11)

Imagine it. The same power that started Jesus' dead heart beating, opened his eyes and strengthened him to push the stone away is at work in every child who calls on the name of the Lord. As parents, we can ask our kids those two questions and then assure them that, though he may work differently or more slowly than they would like, the living God is working supernaturally in their life, day by day, helping them. We can promise them that the change that feels impossible, and indeed is impossible for *them* to achieve, is achievable. They can be confident that they are not stuck—that they can get there.

I remember a conversation I had with a Christian counsellor. He worked for a day a week with those in our church who had gone through trauma or who struggled with addictions. In terms of our pastoral structures, he was the last in the line. "How do you cope with the responsibility?" I asked him. "What if you can't help? There is no one after you!" He paused. (First tip for counselling: take a breath and pause. It gives you instant gravitas.) Then he said, "What you're forgetting, Ed, is that with the Lord, change is inevitable".

I love that word "inevitable". It means guaranteed, certain, beyond doubt. No exceptions.

Every Christian parent will see change in their family because God is at work. It might not be the change they were hoping for, in the way they were hoping for, at the speed they were hoping for. It may be that the Spirit goes to work on their heart before their kid's heart. It may be that the Spirit goes to work on their kid's heart in a way that no one can see—at least, not for years. But with the Lord, change is *inevitable*. Through prayer and because of the work of the Spirit, your character (and therefore, growing from your character, your behaviours) are being changed to make you more like Christ.

So, instead of carrying around a mental list of ways in which you wish your kids would behave differently, carry around a prayer that the Spirit would be at work in their hearts. And as you pray that, pray he would also be at work in *your* heart.

The goal of parenting is to witness to our children about Jesus and, if the Lord works to bring them to faith, to then disciple our own brothers and sisters in Christ. In any other discipleship relationship, we would be embarrassed to adopt nagging, shouting and despair as our chief tools. That is a discipleship course that no one needs! And in any other discipleship relationship, we would expect and accept that we have much to learn too—that both of us are a work in progress. It's no different in parenting. I am convinced that parenting is where most (or all?) of us will see the greatest change to our hearts. Nothing reveals our anger, impatience or selfishness like being a parent. Parenting confronts us with our need to change, even as we seek to lead our kids to change. And it is always the Holy Spirit who brings that change.

IT TAKES A CHURCH TO RAISE A CHILD

There was some research published in 2011 in the USA that wanted to understand what could be done about the fact that half of the teens who grew up in Christian homes had stopped attending church by the time they left secondary school. The hope was to find out what could make the faith of our children stick into their adult years, so the research was called *Sticky Faith*.[3] A key finding was that every child needs five adults to be involved in their spiritual lives. The data showed that the African proverb is true—it does take a village to raise a child; or rather, it will take your church to raise your child.

On a podcast for parents that I host, Marìna explained that she had gone to church with her two teenage children the previous Sunday knowing that they were all fed up with

---

3 Chap Clark and Kara E. Powell, *Sticky Faith: Everyday Ideas to Build Lasting Faith in Your Kids* (Zondervan, 2011).

each other. She pushed them through the door and said, "Talk to anyone". She was at the end of herself: they had stopped listening, so they now needed to choose anyone else in the church to talk to. Marìna had total confidence that it didn't matter who they chose. They could be totally honest about how they were feeling and what they were thinking about their mum. She trusted everyone in her church family to offer them care, wisdom and grace. That is a healthy church! That is the kind of church Paul called the Ephesians to be, and calls us to be:

> Be completely humble and gentle; be patient, bearing with one another in love. Make every effort to keep the unity of the Spirit through the bond of peace. There is one body and one Spirit, just as you were called to one hope when you were called; one Lord, one faith, one baptism; one God and Father of all, who is over all and through all and in all. (Ephesians 4:2-5)

The work of the Spirit in our lives is wrapped up with the "us" of church. The Spirit gives us unity to trust together in Jesus Christ. He works to produce patience and love for one another instead of just superficial or polite friendship. The one Spirit works to produce in us the same hope for our future, when his good work in us will be complete.

The normal way the Spirit works practically in our lives is not by removing us from the problems we are in but by placing God's people in them with us. As a parent, allow yourself to be vulnerable and rely on your church. I can remember those moments when I have relied on our church in our moments of need:

- Sitting with an older couple in our first month of parenthood, feeling worried and with my wife in tears, as they reassured us that we were doing fine and that the Lord has us.

- Being visited at home by an older mum in the congregation to help my wife with breast feeding (never has a natural bodily function been so very difficult to make work adequately).

- Being asked by a younger man if he could take my son for a walk during the church youth camp to talk about how his faith and life were going. I think I responded like an enthusiastic puppy: "Yes please. Yes please. Yes please. Thank you. Thank you. Thank you."

- Walking with a father from church as we tried to help each other to navigate our daughters' complicated friendship (and, wow, my daughter's friendships seem very, very difficult to me).

And I can look back on memories of precious moments when I felt like I could actually play my part in loving other families in church:

- I had just told my little Sunday School group that their behaviour the week before had not been good enough; one 5-year-old boy, who was often in trouble, looked into my eyes and said, "Was it me again?" It felt like a privilege to tell him that it was not just him, and that he could have a fresh start because we believed in forgiveness.

- The 7-year-old girl who asked me if her grandad was in heaven. Her mum wanted to sit in on the conversation as I asked the girl what she knew about heaven. Praying together at the end was precious.

- The 11-year-old boy who I played (terrible) football with as he continued to cope with his dad living abroad and showing little interest in him.

- The-16 year-old boy who said that his dad was disappointed with him. I held back tears as we sat down and opened the Bible together for reassurance.

- The 17-year-old girl who told me about the lesson that week on using pronouns: "I know how to use pronouns!" She was on the edge of tears. It was great to agree that she did know how to care for those friends who wanted to change their gender identity, and that it was possible to be caring without having to affirm all their choices, and that real care was not about the use of pronouns.

HOW TO RESPOND TO BAD BEHAVIOUR

Every parent wants their children to behave well. A Christian distinctive is that we believe it is a work of the Spirit over many years, usually through the words and prayers of a parent, in partnership with the local church. A Christian distinctive is that we care more about the heart than the conduct—that we want to raise kids who are confident that they're forgiven by Christ and that his Spirit is at work in them, rather than raising little Pharisees who behave well, especially when others are watching, and are proud that they're good.

Consider how you normally respond to your child's bad behaviour. Most of us have a method we usually fall back on.

- If we threaten our child (perhaps by shouting at them), "You do not want to find out what I will do to you next..." then we are trying to control their behaviour with *fear*. One day they will not be afraid of us anymore. It is right to tell our kids what to do and expect obedience, especially in the earlier years. But we should do that without frightening them. We should do that by gently explaining to them that God has placed us in loving authority over them, to help them see that, imperfect as we are, it is good to live under loving authority, because we all live under his.

- If we only offer rewards and punishment— "If you stop lying for a month, I will get you a new bike"; "Do that again and we will go home"—we are seeking to prompt better behaviour through *manipulation*. One day we will no longer be able to punish them, and our rewards will become inadequate. Rewards can be good. God is kind to us. We can reward our children. But let's reward them for patterns of godly behaviour or milestone achievements rather than as a constant form of behaviour manipulation. Yes, punishment is sometimes necessary, and there are many options that will help the child to understand that their behaviour has consequences. But remember that as your child gets older, punishment becomes less effective as a method for helping them to learn. Seek to praise and reward their character rather than only ever their behaviour or their achievements.

- If we make them feel guilty for the effect on us of their bad behaviour—"Do you know how tired I am? Do you know what you are doing to me?"—then we are seeking to modify their conduct by creating *shame* in them. Eventually, we would love them to know with certainty that they need feel no shame for their sin. In Christ they have freedom from shame. We also believe that shame is a right response to sin. It is a God-given blessing to help bring us to the cross. But we should not weaponise that blessing.

Parenting is hard! When you're tired or busy or stressed, it is always going to be easier to seek to moderate behaviour than shape the heart. It's easier to stick strawberries onto an apple tree than to plant and water and prune and wait for a strawberry plant to grow and bear fruit. But "a good man brings good things out of the good stored up" in his heart (Matthew 12:35)—so take the time to parent, and commit to praying for, your kids' hearts. Your conversations, the church's partnership and God's powerful work are enough.

Do not be tempted to think, "The Spirit doesn't work". Don't aim for the heart for a few weeks, see little progress, and give up. Imagine your child's godliness (and yours) as tracing the path of a yoyo as you walk up some stairs. You would see it rise and fall. With each rise there can be elation. With each fall there can be despair. But over the years, there is a clear rise from the ground floor to the first floor.

Don't forget that with the Lord, change is inevitable. And it's the heart where the Lord goes to work.

Questions to think about...

1. Do you tend to default to fear, manipulation or shame to change your child's behaviour? Why is that, do you think? How would you like to approach things differently?

2. Can you see a repeated wrong behaviour or sadness in your child? What might lie behind that behaviour or sadness? (It may be helpful to ask: What is their heart craving? What is their heart afraid of? What is their heart wrongly believing?) Is there a conversation you could have to help them start a slow, steady, Spirit-fuelled change in their heart?

3. Is there someone in your church who is a role model or a positive influence on your child? Do they know that?

6

I KNOW WHAT TO DO
WHEN I'M NOT OK

The tears come at school drop-off. The sweetest little boy, with a mop of wild hair, runs excitedly along... but his legs are running too fast for his body, and there's the awful moment when you know he's about to fall. Then comes the sound of knees hitting concrete. The pause. The scream. Every parent steps towards him, hands out, gasps of sympathy, longing to fix it, wipe the tears and take away the pain.

The tears come just before bed. Your 10-year-old daughter is tired. You're tired. She says through moist, sad eyes imploringly fixed on you, "I don't want to go to school tomorrow". There is a long pause. You're the parent: you're meant to be able to stop the tears. You know she still doesn't have a single friend in school. You've had this conversation so many times before. The tears still come.

Then the tears seem to be replaced by silence in the teenage years. Time alone in their bedroom. Time without talking at the table. Questions seem to cause more anger than honesty. When once you felt like you had tools at your disposal for fixing their problems, now you're not even sure you know what the problems are.

How many of our *own* problems (as adults and parents) are we able to fix? If we dare to consider our own problems— the ones that cause the repeated heartache, the greatest soul-searching and the tears—we realise that *fixing* problems is rarely straightforward.

Tears are a part of life. We live in a broken world. Our beautiful perfect world only lasted for two pages of the Bible story. Since Genesis 3, sin and its effects have infected, filled and ruined our world.

Every single aspect of every single life is affected. Nothing quite works how it should. In the small details, the shine seems to always be removed. It might be the rare moment of success that is spoilt by the cutting, jealous words of a friend, or the exciting school trip that is missed because of the freak vomiting bug. But the brokenness is also in the large, suffocating situations that can dominate our children's lives. The young life that is torn apart by a rare illness. The family constantly fighting against the claustrophobic limitations of unemployment and poverty. The gifted, talented teenager crushed by depression and self-harm.

We'd love to protect our children from pain and to save them from hurt. It's why we buy stairgates, hold their hands as they learn to walk and teach them how to cross the road. Most of us have an instinct to wrap them in cotton wool, to protect them from all harm and to sweep all obstacles from the path in front of them. But then no one would ever learn to ride a bike, take a risk or test their limits. No one would learn from their mistakes or feel freedom.

Our heavenly Father says he is a better parent than any of us (Luke 11:11-13). He is much more realistic about the world we live in than we sometimes are, and he is far closer to our children than we can be. He does not promise to clear every obstacle from their paths (or ours); in fact, he warns us that obstacles will regularly appear (for instance, Romans 8:17-18; 2 Timothy 3:12). This doesn't reduce his compassion. He is not standing far off and rolling his eyes when we flounder and are surprised that things are hard, as if to say, *Seriously? You should have seen this coming.* Instead he is right alongside us as the obstacles hit, leaning in to help us and to encourage us to trust him.

Every parent in that playground was ready to step in for that little boy. We knew that he was shocked and hurting, and needing to feel safe. What would we do as his parent? We would wrap our arms round him, hold him close, tell him, "I'm here" and "I love you", and hold him until the shock and pain eased. We'd fix him up, brush him down, set him back on his feet... and we'd be ready for the next fall.

Our God does the same.

JESUS IS HERE

Jesus' friend Lazarus was very ill when Mary and Martha sent word to Jesus to come immediately to heal their brother (John 11:1-3). They already knew who Jesus was, and so they summoned the only one with the power of the living God to come to their dying brother's bedside. In this sense, this is our story too. We believe that Jesus still has all power over every moment and every situation. The difference is that he is no longer in the next province, state or county. We can't stick a stamp on a letter for it to arrive in his hand. Instead he is in God's throne room, reigning now and for ever. Instead of a stamp, we know that our prayers go straight into that throne room. But still, if we share Mary and Martha's faith, we can watch and learn, because if the day comes when we have nowhere else to go (and I suggest that it will for all of us), we need to know what to expect from God.

It doesn't appear to start well. After receiving the message, Jesus delayed leaving—by days, not hours (v 6-7). By the time he arrived, Lazarus had been dead for four days. In terms of urgent medical help being delayed, this feels like the nightmare scenario!

When Jesus met Martha, he understood her heart, listened to her questions and knew exactly what she needed in that moment. Her world was shaking, her faith was wobbling and she needed Jesus to remind her of the anchor she had. "I am the resurrection and the life. The one who believes in me will live, even though they die ... Do you believe this?" (v 25-26). *Hold tight, Martha, to what you know. Focus on your great hope even though circumstances scream that things are hopeless.*

"Yes, Lord," she replied, "I believe that you are the Messiah, the Son of God, who is to come into the world." (v 27)

Here is Martha finding her footing in the sinking sand. Here is the anchor holding her fast in the storm. Here is faith in suffering. Isn't this what a Christian parent hopes for themselves and their children in suffering? That they will place their trust in an eternal King who will never leave them, who has all power, who can be trusted, whose loving arms are wrapped around them *in that moment*, even though their heart is aching, their tears are flowing and their future feels broken?

It is possible. I have some friends with a teenage daughter with a chronic, complex illness. Her pain has recently been relentless. Her everyday life has been severely disrupted. For the moment, all her hopes for her future have been smashed. As is the way with complex illnesses, the family have been passed from one specialist doctor to another as they seek to understand the connection between the symptoms and the causes. One senior psychiatric doctor asked for a meeting with the parents on their own. They were hopeful that it was to tell them definitively what was wrong with their daughter. The doctor had a different agenda: "Your daughter is in severe, relentless pain, but she remains joyful despite her suffering. Can you explain how that is possible?"

They explained that their daughter, like them, is a Christian, and the Bible's message is that a deep joy is possible even in the worst of suffering because God remains close, loving and actually helping. The doctor was surprised and asked where exactly in the Bible it says that. They showed the doctor Psalm 23:

> The LORD is my shepherd, I lack nothing ...
> Even though I walk
>   through the darkest valley,
> I will fear no evil,
>   for you are with me. (Psalm 23:1, 4)

The doctor immediately followed up with "And where else does it say this?" So they walked her through more passages—those they had raised their daughter to believe, preparing her for the day when they would not be able to remove her from the suffering. What a Bible study! They may have left without a diagnosis, but they left a doctor who had heard about Jesus and, crucially, seen the difference he makes, and so I imagine they walked away with a fresh sense that Jesus is the Messiah, the one whom their child could trust despite the uncertainty.

What faith! Why not pause and pray now, "Lord, when my child's suffering comes, may they have that joy caused by the certainty of knowing that their good shepherd walks with them through the valley of the shadow of death. Amen."

JESUS WEEPS

When Jesus arrived at Mary and Martha's home, he knew that his carefully timed arrival would mean that he could do more than heal Lazarus; he could raise him from the dead, "so that you may believe" . With all this knowledge and clarity, how did Jesus respond to the wave of grief and loss he found at the family home? Did he confidently stroll in, smiling in the midst of the questions and the tears, saying, *I know exactly what I'm doing. It's going to be fine. Pull yourselves together!*

No.

Jesus wept.

He was upset. He was moved. He was gripped by the shared grief of the tearful gathered friends. He shared their grief. He felt grief. He was one of us. There is a profound simplicity in Jesus mirroring their emotions—a deep connection. He feels it. His tears remind a non-verbal child that her inner tension is understood; she can uncoil and know the peace of Christ. The pacing parent of a struggling newborn can breathe again. The weight in our chest can be lifted by looking into our Saviour's tears and knowing that he gets it. The one who perfectly bears the Father's image also bears ours.

THE BATHROOM FLOOR

I have been reliably informed by several teenagers that the bathroom is the best place in the house to head to for a cry. There's probably a lock on the door, and you can hide away, run the tap to mask the sniffing or sobbing, and stare sadly into the mirror at the face looking back at you that understands how you feel.

A friend told me of the moment in her teenage years when she came home from youth group, totally heartbroken by a double betrayal: she'd been dumped for her best friend. "I'm going to wash my hair," she said, and headed to the bathroom to crumple onto the floor and weep. But mums just know—and her mum just knew. There came the gentlest of knocks on the bathroom door: "Can I come in?" The door opened, and Mum sat on the edge of the bath, stroked her hair, and with tears in her eyes told the story of her own teenage heartbreak. In that moment, the divide narrowed as her daughter realised that her mother had once been a teenager just like her and that (unbelievably) she'd been dumped too! She too had cried in a bathroom; she too had been let down by her friends. She understood. She had been there. She could tell her what helped.

Well, Jesus has wept. Jesus has seen grief and pain and death, and he's wept over it.

Jesus has, if you like, sat on the bathroom floor of our sorrow. Whatever it is that reduces your children to a crumpled heap, he's been there. Whatever might lead them to screaming questions and slamming doors, he's known the pain. This is the wonder of the incarnation: that God took on human form and, in the person of Jesus Christ, came right in to feel what we feel and face what we face. He is no detached observer. He experienced a toddler's frustration, a child's curiosity, a teenager's emotions, an adult's disappointment. He's closed the divide, he understands, and he knocks on the door of our heartache and offers more than sympathy because he offers what helped him in those moments to keep trusting and clinging to faith, hope and love. Jesus is able to offer a deeper help than the best parent or closest friend ever could because he fully understands and he completely knows. And he knows, even if we don't, what to ask his heavenly Father for that will help us in that moment.

Not only that, but he came to do more than simply understand and cry with us. He came to save our children. He experienced the same rejection that they may feel in the playground, but he suffered that so that they need never be rejected by God. He experienced the same condemnation in court that they might feel in their failures, but he suffered that so that they need never be condemned by God. He experienced the same pain of the worst illness or accident they will endure, but he suffered that so that they need never be punished for their sins. He knows what those experiences are like. In his loving rescue, there can be help for their suffering right now.

In the lonely isolation of depression, the cross is the ultimate shout of "I love you".

In the hurtful rejection by children in the playground, the cross is the ultimate shout of "You matter to the King."

Our children do not have to wait for Christ's return to experience the benefits of Christ's death for them. We can speak his suffering into their present suffering— we can remind them that Jesus understands them, and that Jesus has triumphed for them, and that Jesus loves them.

WHO DO YOU CALL?

When you are in tears, who do you turn to? When life feels unfair or a crisis hits, what do your children see you do next? Perhaps you turn to those who you think will understand—your closest friend, a family member or your other half. Perhaps you turn inward, grit your teeth, and resolve to get through. Perhaps you fall apart.

What stops you from coming to Jesus? Do you think he doesn't understand you? "Perfect Jesus can't identify with messed-up me." Or do you think he won't help? "It's too insignificant, too far from his area of interest, or too far beyond his power to fix me." "Look how badly I've responded to this—I can't ask Jesus to help me now." Remember who Jesus is. In his compassion, he wants to help, and in his power, he is able to help.

Jesus cares, and he can help you because he has conquered all the things that you can't. He resisted temptation, he carried on trusting, he endured death and he rose—all for you. Now Jesus stands in heaven, praying for you (Hebrews 7:25). He knows what to ask for, even when you don't, because he understands how you feel and what you need. So go to him to be understood. Don't turn only to your friends or family but to Jesus, your Saviour.

And as we learn to run to him, we'll learn to take our kids to him.

It is one thing to go to our Saviour open-handed with nowhere else to go—it is another to go there with our child. When your child is in tears, they have come to you for a reason and a solution. It can feel like passing the buck to take their problem to Christ. You know there will be a moment when you have both said, "Amen", when you look into one another's eyes, and you see your child's next question in their expression: "Now what? Surely that prayer wasn't all you've got?"

I have a friend who was diagnosed with cancer when she had three children in primary school. Her instinct in those long months of treatment was to feel that she was failing her family by not being the reliable rock on which her family was built. How could her children look to her for strength and certainty when she knew nothing about her future? She learned in that experience that she had never been the rock for her family that she was trying to be. She had always tried to point them to God as their better parent. Now there was no debate about where their certainty and security would need to come from. Ultimately, they needed God, not her. They needed to pray together for her health. They needed to rest her life in his safe, loving hands. That is faith. She now (healthily) remains committed to that principle and is thankful for the opportunity to have learned her lesson in front of her watching children.

It is normal to struggle to know what to say to your children in the darkest moments. My friend remembers that it was another Christian who sat with her whole family the night before her operation and read a psalm to them. The usual way that God helps us in our darkest moments is by placing another Christian to be in our darkness with us. Do not wait for your own family to be suffering before you speak words of Christ's comfort to hurting children. Search for the family who need you to do it for them.

I do not know how any parent can raise their children without a good church. I remain baffled by the family I used to know who turned down their church's offer of a rota of home-cooked food after the birth of their son. I suspect they felt that their wealth meant that they shouldn't need the love of others. But they prevented their church from being family to their new son. Be sure to welcome others who are ready to step into your difficulties and darkness to offer real care and words of biblical truth.

Your suffering is always an opportunity to show your children what you know is true of God. We have a large, strong, athletic father of two boys in our church. In his company, I feel a little inadequate! Following a series of sudden medical crises, he was diagnosed with an illness that required an operation on a vital organ. He was wonderfully honest with the church. We prayed for him. I was chatting to his wife in the week of the operation. "Has he prayed about this with his sons?" I asked. He hadn't. This was an opportunity. These boys had only known their dad as a dependable rock. It might be humbling, but this was a wonderful chance to show them that their dad is weak, but that they have a stronger heavenly Father who will never grow old, who will never be diagnosed with an illness, and who will never be nervous about his ability to provide for his family.

The stronger we are, the wealthier we are, the more independent we are, the harder it is to kneel next to our children and point them to someone else. But this is what faith does. Faith looks like accepting that we cannot be all that our kids need, and pointing them to another, and trusting that he'll come through for them. Perhaps this is hardest for men because we have an instinct deep in us to be the final protector and source of strength. But the greatest protection we can offer our children is to put our arm around them, pray together and offer them to the Lord's care.

TOO GOOD TO BE TRUE?

Parenting so often brings us to the end of our own resources. I think of the son of my friend Claire. He has had a complex story so far and, as a result, is going through huge struggles with his mental health. He lashes out, blaming his family and destroying their home. There have been over a hundred acts of destruction, representing thousands of pounds of damage. The emotional cost can't be so easily calculated.

When Claire is on her knees picking up the pieces again, embarrassed to tell her well-meaning friends that "No, it isn't better", she has a God who does not stand at a distance offering platitudes. No, she has a Saviour who weeps with her at the brokenness of life and who offers her in that moment the strength to keep trusting and to keep going. Claire works through the medical appointments, the counselling sessions, the social-services meetings and the suggestions that keep coming at her. She knows that her family's story is unlikely to change overnight.

She keeps running to Christ. She is hard-pressed but not broken. She is not certain of her son's recovery, but she is certain of Christ's faithfulness. That is faith, and I'm in awe of her.

When I go for a walk with her son, I realise that I do not understand the causes, I cannot fix it and I must not offer simple answers. (He has heard too many of those.) Instead, my role is to say, with confidence, that there is one who does understand him, who can help him, who can use the hardest of situations for good, and who will one day fix all things. Faith and patience are needed. I have learnt to pray with him for self-control (because the Spirit promises to grow this in those are trusting in Christ). That prayer feels like a risk. His struggle has lasted years, and he would be the first to say that God has not answered that prayer so far (that he can see). When we doubt that God has the power to change the story, we remember that Lazarus walked from the tomb. We remember that Jesus questioned and cried in the Garden of Gethsemane as he walked his own agonising path. We remember that he cried out both "Why have you forsaken me?" (Matthew 27:46) and "Father, into your hands I commit my spirit" (Luke 23:46) from the cross, and that he walked out of the grave so that one day we will do the same.

EXPECT TEARS

This is a book about identity. And suffering is part of a Christian's identity. That is a difficult truth for Christian parents to face. Suffering is going to be part of the story of our children's lives if they seek to follow Christ. Not only do they live in a broken world, and so they will face frustration and brokenness because of that, but they will have to face the rejection of a sinful world and see it written on the face of their friends and hear it in the taunts of those they want to like them. God offers an adventurous faith-filled life, but he does not offer us an easy one. Jesus did not make exceptions, even for your child, when he said, "In this world you will have trouble" (John 16:33). Don't see suffering for your child as a disaster or a deviation from how life should be. Be ready for it. Expect it. And make sure that in it, you point them to their Saviour and pray that God would use it to show them their need of him and to make them more like him. Remind them that we *have* been promised a life without tears, an end of illness and death, and a place where all brokenness will be put back together, but that life is in the new creation—it is not yet.

As a parent, our instinct is to choose the path of least resistance and least pain for our children. The decision to let our children risk some measure of hurt so that they can learn is always difficult for a parent. But to encourage our children to pursue a Christian life is to know that in this world a life with less comfort lies ahead. This is not cruel. We are certain that the sacrifice is worth it for the life to the full that Christ offers *now* (John 10:10), as well as the wonderful eternal life that Christ offers after his return (Revelation 21:4). Christian parents are loving their children by wanting them to live for Christ, but they are not giving their children comfort and ease by calling them to live for Christ. To commend this life to our children means we must be ready to train them for the inevitable suffering (and to model in our own lives the reality that Christ-likeness and comfort don't often go together).

There will be tears. Life is about working out what to do when you fall—when you fall from a tree, when you forget your lines when you stand on the stage, when your mistake brings defeat on the sports pitch, when you spend your money on the wrong thing, when you say the wrong thing in the crucial interview, when you receive the diagnosis from the doctor, when you lose friends because you stand by what Jesus says, when your own sin wrecks things. Parenting involves allowing our kids to take risks and make mistakes and be hurt, and loving them and helping them learn through it all.

Christian parenting involves walking with our kids through the suffering and pointing them to their good Shepherd throughout, because the purpose of our parenting is for the day when we are not there. Then, we pray, they will continue to look to their good Shepherd so that, when they walk through the darker valleys of life and even of death, our children's faith in him enables them to smile in the tears and say with confidence:

Surely your goodness and love will follow me
all the days of my life,
and I will dwell in the house of the LORD for ever.
(Psalm 23:6)

Questions to think about...

1. What suffering makes you want to ask God, "Why?"

2. What part of your family life prompts the most tears? How do you react?

3. How could a conversation in the midst of the tears be changed by Jesus' tears with Mary and Martha?

7

I AM WONDERFULLY MADE

I didn't see it coming.

We were driving past cows. I told the children that, as a boy, my family had cows. I said that each year they had calves.

Then the question came from the back seat: "Where did the calves come from?"

Silence. I realised what I had done. I had caused our first conversation about sex. I kept my eyes on the road. I felt panicked. Children smell panic. I considered my options. I took a deep breath. I was going to have to tell the truth. I was about to say the words "willy" and "sex" in the same sentence, and, on this occasion, I had to not laugh. I had no time to draft potential answers. Could I distract them with the sudden sight of a bird of prey? Could I phone my mum for advice? *Pull yourself together, man. You know this stuff. Mostly.*

I began, slowly... "If you put a bull in a field with cows..."

"Yes, Dad?"

I wanted to shout, "Would you please give me a moment? This is really difficult for me. I've never done this before."

I continued. "... he has sex with all the cows in the field. That means, with each cow, he puts his willy in their vagina."

I had done it. But now, how could I link this to men and women? It suddenly dawned on me that one bull having sex with every cow in the field was not the perfect parallel for the Christian approach to sex. I kept talking. I tried to sound relaxed and experienced because I knew that our tone in parenting usually says more than our words. I can't remember what I said next.

I survived to fight another day. Many more conversations have happened since then. I have learnt a little more about the human body and Christian sexual ethics, but mainly I have learnt that, as a parent, I am the front line. I need to be the one to have conversations with my children. The list of topics feels really intimidating (and so we'll be taking the next three chapters to think about them): the biological differences between boys and girls, the names of body parts, relationships, puberty, masturbation, sexuality, sex, marriage, friendship, body image, gender dysphoria... I could go on. I would happily go through my whole life without discussing some (or all) of those topics. But I am a Christian parent, so I must not allow my children's school or friends or favoured social-media influencers to tell them what they need to understand to live a flourishing life. I am also certain that the Lord's grace is sufficient. He is with me as I take tentative steps, one conversation at a time.

And he's with you.

WORSHIP YOUR BODY OR HATE YOUR BODY?

Our culture has a difficult relationship with our bodies. We seem to value them highly, parading them (photoshopped) on social media, lavishing them with cosmetics, sculpting them in the gym, or having surgery to match the images we see on our screens. Yet at the same time society responds with affirmation to people who feel they are "trapped in the wrong body", as if our bodies were separate from our "real" selves. We are encouraged to disconnect our bodies from who we are:

- Sex is treated as just a bodily activity, like drinking a protein shake, running on a treadmill or having an injection. If that is true, then we can sleep with whoever we like, when we like, without limit. Our culture advises us to not get emotionally involved with those we have sex with. We call it "friends with benefits" to make it sound like we're lending money or sharing a car. In some children's resources, sex is described as "something done by two adults to give each other pleasure".[4] That puts it in the same category as going for a walk in the hills or having a milkshake with friends. The

---

4 "What Kids Want to Know about Sex and Growing Up", Children's Television Workshop, 1992; quoted in Nancy R. Pearcey, *Love Thy Body* (Baker, 2019), p 28.

heart and soul has been removed from the physical activity. When the act finishes, when the pleasure ends, apparently we can walk away without any lasting consequences.

- The transgender movement wants to disconnect the body from the person. The body is described like an incidental piece of clothing that may or may not fit properly. We are told that gender is *your internal sense* of being a man or woman, which you then express externally, while sex is *how your body is categorised* because of genitals and chromosomes. The "true self", the trans movement preaches, is your internal feeling, and the body is something that can be adjusted to come into line with your true self.

- Our culture has idolised the outward appearance, divorcing it from the inner self. The cosmetics, bodybuilding, plastic-surgery and anti-aging industries all aim to enhance the outer appearance without reference to the authenticity of the person. Curation of our bodies matters far more than character, and we lie about the outward appearance, photo-shopping every advertising image so that it is no longer a picture of a specific individual.

As Christians, perhaps we have spent too much time saying what is wrong with our culture's direction of travel, and our children have heard us as simply saying "no" in a world that seems to be saying "yes". The truth is, we have a better story, a positive story, to tell about our bodies, about sex and about gender. In this chapter, we're going to think about how to celebrate our bodies; in the next, about how to help our kids think about sex, marriage and friendships; in the one after that, about how to think about gender.

OUR BODIES ARE US

The Bible says that the body and the person are one.

> *Then the LORD God formed a man from the dust of the ground and breathed into his nostrils the breath of life, and the man became a living being. (Genesis 2:7)*

When Adam was created, life was breathed into the body. It is not that there was a "real" Adam who was placed into a suitable body. His body was a part of what made him him. Nor was it that the "real" Adam was merely his body, a collection of atoms. His body was just a *part* of what made him him.

The same is true of us…

> *Do you not know that **your bodies** are temples of the Holy Spirit, who is in **you**, whom you have received from God? **You** are not your own; **you** were bought at a price. Therefore honour God with **your bodies**.*
> (1 Corinthians 6:19-20, emphasis added)

Look how Paul uses both "your bodies" and "you". You and your body cannot be separated. And as Christians, our bodies are as precious as the Most Holy Place in the Old Testament—the place at the heart of the temple where God dwelled among his people—because, by his Spirit, God himself lives in us. That is very hard to teach to children (and hard for us to understand), but what is clear is that to be a human is to have a body; and to be a Christian is to have a very precious, even holy, body.

OUR BODIES ARE AMAZING

For you created my inmost being;
*   you knit me together in my mother's womb.*
I praise you because I am fearfully and wonderfully made;
*   your works are wonderful,*
*   I know that full well.*
My frame was not hidden from you
*   when I was made in the secret place,*
*   when I was woven together in the depths of the earth.*
*   (Psalm 139:13-15)*

When they were little, my mother-in-law knitted jumpers for my children. I love thick knitted jumpers. I made my jealousy of my kids' jumpers clear. And many Christmases later, I unwrapped my first hand-knitted jumper. It meant so much to me. Creativity and love had been invested in making something just for me. A total one-off. Unrepeatable.

Our bodies are each a unique work of craftsmanship. Every detail has been chosen to be just that way, matched exactly with our needs, given by the one who loves us the most. You are not a shiny mass-produced piece of technology. You were knitted together, personally and uniquely, by a loving Creator. So were your children.

"I praise you because I am fearfully and wonderfully made; your works are wonderful, I know that full well." The genius artist has declared that your body is "wonderfully made". Rather than disputing his verdict, let's praise him.

Thankfulness brings joy and celebration. Thankfulness drives out insecurity, unhelpful comparison and complaint. Modern mental-health advice for parents is to foster gratitude in our children. If we keep searching for a way to be thankful, it changes our mood; it changes our attitude to our situation and it allows us to make progress. Christians know who to thank! "I praise you because I am fearfully made."

We need to help our children thank God for their incredible bodies. That's easier when they're younger. I will miss the day when I can no longer thank God for my youngest child's body in our special way. We close our eyes. I thank God for his incredible knees that allow him to jump, as I squeeze his knee cap. I thank God for his arms that allow him to hug, as I tickle his armpits. I thank God for his feet that allow him to stand strong in high winds as I tickle his toes. I love our wriggly, giggly prayers together.

I thank God with my older son as we walk to a sports match he is playing in. Sometimes he gets nervous that he will let his team down. Sport can do that. We thank God for his incredible body, which allows him to run and compete. We thank God that he has such an amazing body that it means he has been selected to play. We pray that he would play sport as an act of worship, humbly giving thanks for what he's been knitted together with the ability to do, and humbly accepting what he's not been knitted together to be able to do.

If only the conversations and prayers remained this simple as our children get older! It is harder to thank God for her body with a teenage daughter who passionately wishes it was different. How do we thank God in a meaningful way as she rolls her eyes? I know what she is thinking: "My body isn't good enough, and you want to give thanks? As if that will help." And yet, I will not stop giving thanks for her body in her hearing. I need her to know that her Creator says its good enough, and that I agree. I have seen enough families struggling with eating disorders. I see the ache in the parents' eyes. There are so many medical steps to take, so many professionals to fight for time with. But we do believe there is one who stands over every medical intervention, and who holds a child's heart and brokenness in his hands as no doctor ever can. I will still pray. May I still read these verses if I am ever in that situation, because these verses will still be true. Every body, however broken, however hated, is fearfully and wonderfully made. I know that because the body's Creator says so in his word. It is his verdict that matters, not our feelings or some friend's Instagram page. Our bodies are amazing because he says so.

OUR BODIES ARE UNSPECTACULAR

Jesus is the perfect human. But look at his body:

> *He had no beauty or majesty to attract us to him,*
> *nothing in his appearance that we should desire him.*
> *(Isaiah 53:2)*

Nothing about his appearance was particularly good-looking. Jesus is the King of all of creation, the absolute pinnacle, the one we will worship without reservation for all eternity... and there was no particular majesty about his appearance.

Jesus probably had some wonky teeth. Maybe his arms were scrawny or his ears stuck out. Jesus was not superficially beautiful, but he too had a hand-crafted, lovingly-made body that was a precious, priceless gift from his Father. God places glory in the ordinary—treasures in jars of clay (2 Corinthians 4:7). His eternal Son had a normal, unremarkable human body. If an unspectacular body was good enough for Jesus, why would we think we need more?

My friend Amy and her family love watersports, so when they're away together, they spend whole days in their wetsuits. Long ago Amy came to terms with the fact that she came more from the drawer labelled "substantial" than "slender". So she had two options—remain on the beach with a book and a flattering outfit or wriggle into an unflattering wetsuit. She decided that her children would prefer to remember more the fun their mum had with them in the sea than how fabulous she looked on the beach.

On one of these wetsuit days, her slim and athletic 12-year-old son looked at her neoprened body and said, "Mum, I wish I looked like you in a wetsuit". The cheek! Except he wasn't joking. "You have a strong body, and no one can push you over," he continued. He wishes his body was powerful. His slim frame feels lacking.

The point is this: we all have hang-ups about our bodies. They're unspectacular in ways that most others seem not to have to deal with. They break in ways we wish they wouldn't. It's important to have conversations about your kids' bodies, and to be careful how you speak about your own body, and to consider what messages you send. Because of the fall, no body is perfect, but King David still thanked God for his. We honour God's handiwork when we enjoy ours, look after it and use it as he intends, avoiding comparison with others.

Our kids need our help to know how best to view their bodies—their amazing yet unspectacular bodies. Most of us can name what we would change about our bodies in a fraction of a second, so our children will probably be the same. Have your answer ready for their disappointment. Ask them what they can do with their bodies that makes them smile. What physical memories stand out for your family? What does your family love doing with your bodies: singing, eating, walking, watching, listening, swimming, dancing, laughing, drinking, running, playing, climbing, diving, spinning? And for those things our child *can't* do because of the body they have been given, gently ask them, "Why do you think God chose it that way? If he knitted together every detail... if he chose to make that part gorgeous... and this part a bit more wobbly, or even broken... how does that help us to understand his love for us? How does that help us to look forward to our future with him when we'll be given perfect bodies? What might he be teaching us?"

We want our children to loudly and regularly hear God's loving statement: *You are fearfully and wonderfully made.* Embracing our bodies as God's good gift to us will transform the way we feel about our own bodies and the way in which we treat other people's. It is not easy, but we need to see the people God made—including our kids, and us—from the perspective of a delighted Creator who wouldn't change a thing more than we view them through the filter of a culture that suggests we should change virtually everything.

OUR BODIES ARE FRAGILE

Superheroes are marked by powerful bodies that can be controlled to achieve *anything*. It is significant that those are the stories that our culture tells our children in films: heroism requires having a powerful, indestructible, young and healthy body.

That is not reality. Our bodies are so frail and so mortal. We start our lives utterly dependent on our mothers and, if we live long enough, we end our lives dependent on the kindness of others. Our fragile bodies have been made that way to shout that we need others to live a flourishing life and to point us to the new creation, when we will have the bodies we long for—without aches, pains or breakdowns.

This is one reason to make sure our children spend time with older, godly Christians. They can learn so much: wisdom, grace and gratitude. They can also see how their bodies will change, even if their minds will feel just as agile and sharp as ever. Our kids need to see that they will not always be young, and that in reality we don't get to live as perpetual 20-somethings in the prime of physical life—and that that's not just inevitable; it's ok. I think heroism looks like an elderly man, frail himself, showing up at his wife's care home day after day, despite the effort it takes, to sit with her and sing the Christian songs of their younger years, which are all she remembers now. I think heroism looks like the older lady in our church who suffers from chronic health issues and whose body keeps failing her, showing up Sunday by Sunday, despite the effort it takes and the exhaustion it produces, because church family matters. I want my kids to see that and notice that and celebrate that too.

OUR BODIES ARE CHANGING

I was recording a podcast for parents. My guest was Dr Liz Jones,[5] and I had asked her to walk through how we talk to our children about their bodies as they go through puberty. My then 9-year-old son was ill in the next room. Afterwards, he said to me, "I heard you say words that I have never heard you say before". As I listen back to that podcast, I can hear in my voice the same quivering tone I used to have as I spoke to my female biology teacher about the human body—a mixture of awkwardness, fear and total confusion. But the thing I learned from Dr Jones

---

5 Liz is a retired doctor, a mother, a grandmother and the founder of Lovewise, which exists to teach children a Christian worldview of bodies, marriage and sex. Faith in Parents: Episode 13a/b https://www.buzzsprout.com/237067/1333870

was this: "Parents are the experts. Don't allow anyone ever to let a parent feel that there is someone more expert than they are at telling their children about these things. A parent knows their child's personality, what they can cope with and their maturity."

Here is a paediatric doctor, a mother and a grandmother telling me that I am best placed to talk to my daughter about her body. Liz could give me a diagram and could teach me some words and help me to say them without blushing, but it is *me and my wife* who are better placed than her to have that conversation with our daughter in a way that will help her to feel more confident about her body and the good gift that it is for her from God.

Dr Jones went on to explain that puberty is God's method of equipping our children to live independent lives and to be able to have a family of their own. Again (and it happened a lot on this episode) I was in awe. Puberty is God's project. He is equipping a child's body with everything needed for adulthood.

Talk to your children about puberty *before* they get there and while they're in the midst of it. The physical changes can be daunting. Hormones are surging, and that changes how children are feeling. At every stage, your children need to know there are people they can talk to— somewhere they can go to share their concerns and dispel the playground myths. Those people should be their parents. You worship the God who invented puberty! If you trust him, then you can be confident and positive as you mention the issues. And mentioning the issues is a great way to prove that there is no list of awkward issues that are off-limits in your home that they'll have to navigate on their own or look to the culture for help with.[6] What could be on that list? Here are a few: height and weight (because, for most of us, the changes rarely take us to where we want to be), acne (which is not a sign of poor hygiene), body odour (which could be), menstrual cycle (which needs to be understood by fathers as well as mothers), body image (which is a cause of anxiety for boys and girls), pubic hair (which is not to be ashamed of), facial hair (because no male is born knowing how to handle a razor), body hair (both the abundance and the scarcity) and peer pressure (the constant pressure to be "normal" when everyone knows deep down that normal doesn't exist).

Part of this involves using words at home that may make us feel awkward. Our kids may also find it hard to use words like "penis" and "vagina", and that's ok. As parents, we do not need to be awkward; instead, let's talk about these things in a straightforward, respectful way. The goal must be that my children hear all of these words from their parent before they are whispered (or shouted) around the playground: vagina, clitoris, hymen, vulva, penis, testes, ovaries, labia, clitoris, scrotum and breasts.

You don't have to make every conversation about puberty a detailed, prepared presentation with colour illustrations (although using at least one of these in each of your kids'

---

6 Rachel Gardner, *The Sex Thing: Reimagining Conversations with Young People about Sex* (SPCK, 2021), p 62.

development would be great). For the most part, it will simply involve taking every opportunity to ask another question, to mention another word or to find out what they already know (or think they do). When you see another billboard plastered with an unreal, idealised, photoshopped body, don't just tut (or stare)—talk about the differences between your bodies and the one on the billboard and, perhaps, the way that images are edited before being shown on billboards and social media. When you watch sport, you can admire the athleticism and the physicality of those bodies, and encourage your children to participate in sport as an activity in which their bodies can be enjoyed, rather than avoid it as an activity in which their bodies are exposed. Enjoy the beauty of human bodies as well as the rest of creation. While we won't want to be gawping at every attractive man or woman who walks past, through the ages some art has understood that the beauty of the human form (in all of its shapes and sizes) is worth admiring carefully *and* then that God is worthy of praise as the ultimate artist.

Here is Rachel Gardner's advice to church youth leaders as their young people go through puberty, which is wise for us as parents to take on board too:

"In times like these, young people growing up in church are most vulnerable to internalizing suggestions that their body is bad and only their spiritual life is pleasing to God. But Jesus is concerned for young people's body hygiene (regularly showering, confident use of menstrual products, washing hands after going to the toilet, etc) as

well as their spiritual hygiene (saying sorry and being forgiven, bringing their cares to God, setting boundaries to limit or prevent access to online sexual images and porn, etc).[7]

Make it your goal to discuss both spiritual and physical things in your home. Neither come naturally to most of us. That doesn't mean we should avoid them. Someone will be teaching your kids about their souls and their bodies. Make sure it's you.

WE NEED TO TALK ABOUT PORN

I remember the planning that went into buying a pornographic magazine with friends when we were about 15 years old. I look back on those days and am amazed at how protected from the harmful effects of porn we were, not because adults stepped up but because the availability and type of images were a world away from the current situation. That magazine was degrading to women and deeply unhelpful for our thoughts. But it was a few dozen pages of photographs, whereas now our children have access to a torrent of hardcore films and images that can be viewed effortlessly. The majority of 11-13-year-olds say they first saw pornography *by accident,*[8] and the average age of children first seeing porn is falling. Generally, pre-pubescent children will be upset or confused by seeing porn, so be gentle with them if it happens. But, more

---

7 *The Sex Thing*, p 64.

8 https://www.bbfc.co.uk/about-us/news/children-see-pornography-as-young-as-seven-new-report-finds (accessed November 21, 2022).

importantly, prepare your kids for it. Ignoring a problem doesn't make it go away.

If you are telling your children the good story about their bodies, then what you say about pornography can fit into this framework. God has made our bodies beautiful. We're not ashamed of them, but we don't let anyone see our special parts, except in our homes when we're in the bath or getting dressed. We take care of them. There are pictures and videos on the internet of naked men and women that take something special and precious and make it cheap. If you see pictures of people without clothes on, remember...

1. Say no. Decide not to look at it. Don't look for longer and don't look for more. There is much more. You can decide not to look at it.

2. Go away. Leave the screen immediately. Do something else to help you to think about other things.

3. Talk to an adult. You can tell us anything. We want to help. We want to know what you have seen. Let's talk it through.[9]

As children get older and go through puberty, you can talk about sexual arousal, wet dreams and bodily responses as the normal response to sexual stimuli. Our bodies' responses to nudity and sexual images are normal and the way God has made us. The challenge with older children is to help them learn how to make godly

---

9 These points are from Patricia Weerakoon, *Talking Sex by the Book* (Growing Faith, an imprint of Anglican Youthworks, 2021), p 85.

decisions. As with so many of God's blessings, misuse and abuse is possible. How sad that one of God's greatest blessings—sex, intimacy and arousal—is so hard to talk about with those we love the most. The tendency of some Christians to remain silent on these things represents an opportunity lost, because sexual intimacy in marriage is an extraordinary blessing whereas sexual sin can cause long-lasting damage. Silence also leads to unnecessary guilt and unhealthy habits, as our children may assume that exploring their bodies is inherently sinful. We need to firmly warn our children away from pornography and be clear with them that it is damaging to those involved in the industry, damaging to our children's relationships and their thought life, and highly addictive. It is the most toxic of combinations: wrong, soul-destroying, easily available and consumed in secret. For myself, I have concluded that the Bible's silence on masturbation[10] should not mean that we are silent. It seems to me that while masturbation can be part of a variety of unhealthy and ungodly habits, it can also be a part of a self-controlled, godly lifestyle. Whatever your own views, be sharing them with your children, as appropriate, when they are starting to understand their sexuality.

It is also good for us to consider our own sexual history and experiences to help us shape, and prompt us to remember the importance of, conversations with our child. Most of us have a mixed bag of past mistakes and accumulated wisdom. Out of love for our children we

---

10 I find Rachel Gardner's insights helpful on this. See *The Sex Thing*, p 67-73.

could revisit our past to support them through a very difficult season of life.

WE CAN DO THIS

I am intimidated by the issues covered in this chapter. I find it hard to have conversations with my children about them. I have learnt to push through the awkwardness with my older children. I need them to know that I *want* to discuss these things. I try to regularly ask questions that mention the issues, even if they don't go further. I recently asked my 15-year-old daughter if her friends were watching porn. She replied, "My friends don't, but others do. Is this going to be a long conversation?" That felt like enough for that moment. We moved on. I hope she knows that I want to help her as it becomes more of an issue, which it will.

Let's also be a force for good in our churches. Our churches need to be places where parents are encouraged to navigate these things, offering them some wisdom in when and how to tackle each topic and partnership in sharing the burden for covering all this ground. Don't hold back from asking older, godly parents for their wisdom. Be willing to share with others what's worked well in your family, and what really hasn't. Ask your preachers and youth leaders to talk about it when it's a relevant application of Scripture. (Two thirds of UK churches said in a survey that they *never* talked to their young people about pornography.[11])

---

11 "Losing Heart", commissioned by Youthscape, 2015.

And let's remember that we have the Spirit of wisdom to help us. We are not sufficient. God is. God can use our mistakes and our failings. He can help us make up for lost time if that's needed. But wherever your kids are at and however things have gone up to this point, remember that learning to navigate these things is one of the many reasons why God puts our children in our homes for so long. Wildebeest jump up seconds after being born and run with the herd—that is not the story with our children. We have time. We have years. There is no rush. Just keep talking. Keep asking questions. Keep listening carefully.

Questions to think about...

1. What do you love about your body? What do you struggle with when it comes to your body? Do the truths we've looked at help you?

2. In what moments does your child use their body to its full ability? How could you grab those moments to thank God with them for their body and its capabilities?

3. Is there a body-related conversation that you unhelpfully avoid having? How could you prayerfully and positively engage your child in that conversation?

8

FRIENDSHIPS, SEX AND MARRIAGE

Lucy was chopping vegetables in the kitchen when her 9-year-old daughter, Holly, said, "Mum, I think I might be bisexual".

Lucy remembers putting down the knife, quietly taking a deep breath and choosing to ignore all the little voices that were screaming in her head. All good so far.

She processed the words that Holly had actually said: "I *think* I *might* be bisexual." *Holly is trying to work something out,* Lucy thought, *and even better, she has decided to come to me with it.*

This is why it is always a good idea for parents to take a breath and count to ten. We choose to love our child by keeping our response calm instead of emotionally (over) reacting. The goal is that next time Holly wants to talk, she knows that Mum is a safe place to go to.

It was time for Lucy to speak, trying to sound calm: "Why do you think that?"

"Well, in school they were talking about different kinds of relationships," answered Holly. "If boys like boys, it's homosexual, and if you like both, it's bisexual. I have friends who are boys and friends who are girls, so I think I'm bisexual."

Lucy made this into a good conversation: "I can see why you would think that. There are different kinds of relationships. You are talking about being a friend, and you want to have all kinds of friends. That is great. When we use a word like 'bisexual' or 'lesbian', we are talking about feelings of sexual attraction, which will happen when you are older. You are a child, and you still have a child's body; your body will change, and your feelings will change. Let's keep talking, but for now, just know that having friends who are both boys and girls is not being bisexual; it's just being a good friend. Does that sound right to you?"

Holly has friends in her class with two mums. The school is helping her to understand the culture she lives in. We might wish it was doing it differently, but her parents are there to help her process what she sees and hears. Lucy is able to help Holly understand her world based on the truth while loving others graciously.

Western culture places great emphasis on sexual attraction being a key part of how we identify: "I am straight / gay / bisexual (delete as appropriate)". This is big for kids, especially teenagers. Danny, aged 13, came home telling his mum that all the boys in his year were saying that they were gay. He explained that it seemed obvious to them because they all preferred hanging out with other boys. Again, this is confusing friendship with sexual attraction, but notice how the whole year-group want to have a label to describe themselves. They are searching for their identity. Teens are also desperate to fit in, worry about upsetting their friends and fear being cancelled, and so our children can be left trying to pick their way across a minefield. Being a Christian and living out Christ's teaching has always been lonely, but perhaps it's especially lonely as a Western teenager in the 2020s. It was not like this for us when we were their age. The rate of change in their culture is dizzying—not just for their parents but for them. One teenage son returned home from school after a discussion about these issues and told his parents, "I struggle to know what clothes to put on in the morning, and you've only just trusted me with a door key—and now I need to choose all my labels! It's just so exhausting."

Our homes need to be places where our children can work these things out safely, admit to anything, ask every question without criticism or fear, and hear truth graciously explained. We have timeless answers in the Bible which will give our children a basis for their thinking and decisions.

THEN GOD MADE FRIENDSHIP

Back in the Garden of Eden, in the moment when Adam had just been created, I imagine him there, a solitary man, clapping his hands purposefully and saying to himself,

So, what now? Where do I start? He would have wanted to fix something, solve a problem, complete a task— anything to escape the reality of being alone. But before he could think through any of this, God stepped in:

> The LORD God said, "It is not good for the man to be alone. I will make a helper suitable for him."
>
> Now the LORD God had formed out of the ground all the wild animals and all the birds in the sky. He brought them to the man to see what he would name them; and whatever the man called each living creature, that was its name. So the man gave names to all the livestock, the birds in the sky and all the wild animals. But for Adam no suitable helper was found. *(Genesis 2:18-20)*

In the midst of all God's good creation, something was "*not* good". Adam's life in the perfect garden wasn't good until he had someone to share it with. The perfect garden was not good without a suitable helper. Adam couldn't enjoy it fully on his own. And no creature measured up.

In my life, at various times, my family has had a dog, a cat, cows and hamsters. Each of them has limited or zero appeal as a suitable helper. Our dog is absolutely loved by all our family, but I am convinced that it's because he never speaks. I can't claim that he actually *helps*. Cows and cats take that silence to another level. They have no need for human owners, except for an occasional feed. Don't get me started on hamsters. They have a deep desire to escape, and eventually do. They are not here to help at all. None of those are adequate.

We are made to have *people* in our lives. We need friends because God made us to love like he does. Having people in our lives is as essential as having air in our lungs.

One of my children has an acute fear of being left alone. When I went to collect a takeaway and left him in the car as I popped in to collect it, he ran in after me in his pyjamas. One minute in the car was too much for him even when he could still see me through the restaurant window. At the start of another school year, when we took him to a church club that he is now old enough to attend, as the end of the club got nearer, he felt scared that he would be left all alone. *I was in the building the whole time, and he knew I was there!* He would be the first to say that it is not good for man to be alone:

> *So the LORD God caused the man to fall into a deep sleep; and while he was sleeping, he took one of the man's ribs and then closed up the place with flesh. Then the LORD God made a woman from the rib he had taken out of the man, and he brought her to the man. (v 21-22)*

God found—God *made*—Adam a "suitable helper". This was not simply another "him". It was someone like him but different, given to be his friend. Let's not miss the fact that before sex, there was friendship, help and care in this marriage.

We are all created for intimacy, which means close, loving friendship. Sexual intimacy is one type of intimacy, but it is not the only type, and it should not even be the most common. We want to raise our children to be in close friendships with people who are different to them.

WHEN THE FRIEND THING IS HARD

In the early years of life, everyone can be friends. When our kids turn 5, often the whole class is invited to the birthday party (which requires those parents to have a particular type of bravery!) Younger children are mostly unaware of differences, just getting on with playing in the mud, kicking the ball and creating the artwork. There's a battle for possession and lots of needing to learn to share as they start to realise that there are others in their world who also have preferences and feelings. "You won't be my friend if..." is the ultimate threat. We can teach children that friendship is our gift to give. We choose to be friends with anyone who needs us. We don't push others out of our game. We include anyone who wants in. Children of this age can welcome and care beautifully.

As we head up the ages, differences become more apparent. A friendship group coalesces because everyone in that group plays the same games, so others are left out. Party invitations become more specific: just this group to the football party; just these few to bowling, painting, or whatever it might be. Groups form. Some children are excluded. If your child easily forms friendships, pray with them that God would point them towards one lonely soul who can be invited into their game. If your child often finds themselves alone, pray with them that they will feel the truth that God never leaves them. Teach them to look at their hand and count the five words with their fingers, "I will be with you" and then make a strong fist, saying, "Joshua 1:5".

By the time kids reach 9-11-ish, a lot of time can be spent in falling out, making friends, pushing others away, competing with one another, and sharing and hearing words of inclusion here and words of exclusion there. It can be cruel, and it often provokes tears.

As parents we need to help our children navigate the messy world of friendships. It is hard to know when to forgive, tolerate and work alongside others. Our children will have many questions (and we will have our own). Do I need to care for someone who has only ever excluded me? Should I be a friend to someone who is always in trouble or will they only be a bad influence? Do I need to keep trying to keep them as a friend if they make me feel bad? These are hard skills to learn. We often won't have the answers. The Bible offers much countercultural wisdom in this area as well as plain common sense. And as ever, when gospel wisdom is combined with our special knowledge of our child, we can have the best conversations with them. Every parent wants their child to have friends. Every parent would like their child to be popular. *Christian* parents might need to care less about their child's friends being different to them. *Christian* parents should want someone else's child to have friends. *Christian* parents will see that popularity was never a goal for Jesus.

We need to help our kids navigate the world of relationships, and first and foremost that means guiding them in their friendships.

I remember the day when a large amount of water was poured into the lap of one of my children in the school canteen (to make it look like they had wet themselves). I found it strange that it was done by a "friend". I found it hard to stomach the detail that a whole group of "friends" had watched, without offering to help. It sounded humiliating and isolating to me. There was so much I wanted to say to my child after school, not all of it printable. There were steps that could be taken—emails that could be sent. But in those moments, what does the gospel say to my child? "God has boundless love and acceptance for you. You are precious. Even if every child in the canteen turned on you, the ruler of the universe still shouts from heaven, *You are mine. I love you.*"

There should be pity for the culprit—they were not made by their Creator to treat others like this. They are the lost soul in need of a Saviour, rather than the enemy to avenge. There can be anger that this was cheered by a crowd. So we can add, "What courage it would take to step out from that crowd and be the friend to someone who is being treated badly. The Bible says that 'a friend loves at all times, and a brother is born for a time of adversity' (Proverbs 17:17). Be sure to be that child if your chance comes."

Popularity in school is rarely linked to the godly, beautiful heart that the Bible commends to our children. When my own child was regularly in tears for a season of their life, without any reliable friends in school, I needed to remember that the fault might not have not lain with them (though it might have). It felt like a real blessing to be able to tell my child about that girl whom I mentioned in chapter 1, who had no friends at 8, and who was still involved in our lives in her twenties, and commend her as the very best of Christian role models. If our children seek to live for Christ, popularity might not follow but we can assure them that they are the winners, even when they can see no evidence of it.

FRIENDS AT HOME

I find it sad to hear from young people in secondary school about how friendship groups usually form along ethnic lines. Black kids hang out with black kids. White kids hang out with white kids. While there may be many reasons why it happens, it is not how God made us to be, and it undoubtedly adds to the inequalities in our communities. Heaven will be a glorious diversity of every colour, culture and nation. In heaven all the English will not be standing awkwardly together in one corner while the dancing Ugandans party together in the centre.

Why are kids like this? The sobering reality of parenting is that lessons are usually caught rather than taught. Our children see what we do before they listen to what we say. So we need to *show* them the value of diverse friendship. Our children will see how we treat others. They will see who we invite to spend time with us. They will see whether we only like people like us. They will hear if we only talk about the easy topics and stay away from the great hurt and pain. I found it sad to hear from a Korean family that they had been in our church for years before they were ever invited into a British home. That should not happen.

My mum is Irish, and she grew up with a constant stream of people coming through her home, telling stories, laughing, arguing and eating together. My dad, who is English and grew up with more of a "my home is my castle; stay out" kind of mentality, says he learnt how to welcome people into our home from her. I grew up with people always welcomed into our home, eating at our table, staying the night and sent off feeling loved. Building friendships as adults often overlaps with hospitality. As Christians we share everything because everything we have is a gift from God. It's nothing to do with impressing people with our homes, our cooking or our children's behaviour. (In fact, my experience is that friends are far more likely to enjoy our care if all three are a bit of a mess!)

There is a gay married couple who we often have in our home. Conversations with our children about sexuality and marriage have happened naturally. As always with younger children, I am nervous that one day an awkward question or a mangled understanding will be blurted out at just the wrong moment, but that's parenting! Hospitality can cross all boundaries. I'd love my children to be able to say that all types of people were welcomed in just the same way. We want those who are not Christians to be welcomed as Christians are.

THE SEX-AND-MARRIAGE PART

In the first chapters of the Bible in the garden, that first friendship became the first marriage: between Adam and Eve, a man and a woman. In the final chapters of the

Bible in the final garden city, there is the final marriage: between Jesus Christ and his church.

I saw the Holy City, the new Jerusalem, coming down out of heaven from God, prepared as a bride beautifully dressed for her husband. (Revelation 21:2)

Christians have every reason to talk to their children about marriage and sexual intimacy because both have been given to us to make sense of our eternity. Marriage has been given to us by God so that we understand his love for us (Ephesians 5:31-32). This blows my mind. Left to me, I would say something like "Marriage has been given by God for sex" or "Marriage is God's basis for society". Both may be true, but the truth is far bigger. We should think of marriage as a committed never-broken passionate relationship that provides a glimpse of how God feels about us, his people.

I once preached at a wedding. To help explain the Bible's view of marriage, I held up an inflatable FA Cup and an inflatable giraffe. No one looked at them and believed that I had been lent the trophy of the oldest football competition in the world or that I was holding an actual giraffe high in the air with my bare hands. They were just models of items far more wondrous and thrilling. There was some similarity between the models and the real things, but no one confused the one for the other. In just the same way, the marriage we were witnessing, with all its romance, beauty and happiness, was a recognisable imitation of the final, eternal marriage. Our marriage to Christ for all eternity is the real thing. He is ours, and we are his. Our marriage with him is for all Christians for ever: no one will feel abandoned, no one will be tempted to walk out and no one will experience the loss of divorce or bereavement. The power of sexual longing and the thrill of sexual intimacy have been planted deep within us to help us feel something of the power and thrill of God's love for us.

This gives us a better story to tell our children about marriage, sexuality and arousal—using, of course, language that is appropriate and comprehensible to their age. At the simplest level, their bodies tell the story very well:

> *"God made us so that men and women have different bodies, picturing the difference between Jesus and us. But he also made us so that men's and women's bodies could fit together in a life-giving closeness, which gives us a picture of Jesus and his church."*[12]

God made each of our bodies definitively male or female (apart from the very small proportion of people born intersex[13]). The ability of a male and female body to fit together and their ability together to produce children is an argument that children can understand for how God

---

12 Rebecca McLaughlin, *Ten Questions Every Teen Should Ask (and Answer) about Christianity* (Crossway, 2021), p 117.

13 "Intersex is a general term for a variety of physical conditions in which a person is born with a reproductive or sexual anatomy that doesn't seem to fit the typical definitions of female or male. The variations in sex characteristics may include chromosomes, gonads, or genitals that do not allow an individual to be distinctly identified as male or female." Andrew Walker, *God and the Transgender Debate* (The Good Book Company, 2022), p 166.

has designed marriage to be between one man and one woman.

Make sure that in your conversations about marriage, you're showing your kids that marriage is special because it's God-given and it's pointing us to how he loves us.

SINGLE PEOPLE CAN GO TO COSTA RICA TOO

Equally, make sure that in your conversations you're showing your kids that not everyone gets married, and that it's no more of a gift than singleness (1 Corinthians 7:7-9, 32-35).

My friend Amy (she of the wetsuit) recently had a 45-minute car journey with her 13-year-old son and 9-year-old daughter. Car journeys are often good for chatting, and that day her son was in the mood to talk. He announced that he had found the perfect destination for his honeymoon—a sloth sanctuary in Costa Rica. It was a light-hearted conversation, so a good time to have a little fun but also to explore his thinking.

"What if the person you are going on honeymoon with doesn't like sloths?" Amy asked.

"Well, then I wouldn't be marrying her," he replied.

"What would matter more—her loving sloths or her loving Jesus?"

"Hmm, she should probably love both."

"And what if you never marry?"

"Well, that would be sad, and I wouldn't have a honeymoon, so I wouldn't get to go to Costa Rica."

"Why could you only go to Costa Rica on a honeymoon?"

"Well, that's the time people have a big holiday."

"You don't have to get married and have a honeymoon to go to Costa Rica to see the sloths. You could just save some money and go. And while it probably would be more fun to go with someone else, you could just go with a friend."

"Or ME!" said his sister: "I like sloths! Let's go together."

"Or me," Amy added. "I'll happily look at sloths in Costa Rica with you if you're paying for us to go."

"Oh, that's true," said her son. "I don't have to get married to go and see sloths."

Amy guided the conversation in a way that helped her kids know that there are different ways in which their lives may pan out. Her son did not need to get married to live a full life. He did not need to find the perfect woman (one who loves Jesus *and* likes sloths). Maybe in a later conversation, she could remind him that if he's friends with Jesus, he is guaranteed the final marriage that will feature far better travels than Costa Rica and even better experiences in God's creation than seeing sloths. There is a marriage for every Christian that satisfies all of our desires, all of our longings and all our unique passions.

MY FRIEND ED

The huge difference between Christ and his church in the final marriage helps us to understand why Christian marriage must be between a man and a woman, not between two men or two women. If I am honest, this is the area I most dread being asked about by friends who are not Christians. Getting in the way of loving relationships does not feel like a Christian instinct. I need people like my friend Ed, who is same-sex attracted, to help me understand how God's story will always be a better story than the one our children are being told in school, in media and by friends:

> "At one level it would be very lovely for me to meet the man of my dreams, get married to him and enjoy being united with him (including sexually). As a result, I find the attempts to justify this within a biblical framework very appealing. But, increasingly, I think this is a false dream because I would be expressing myself sexually in a way that God has not intended, and so damaging all those involved."[14]

When he speaks on sexuality, Ed is asked questions by Christian parents. While they always smile and take care with their wording, the underlying questions are often basically "How can I make sure my child doesn't grow up gay?" and "I fear my child is gay—what can I do about it?" Ed speaks movingly about the two biggest ways in which God has drawn him close and changed him to trust in Christ: in the death of his baby sister when he was a child and in his sexuality. Both have caused him to go regularly to his heavenly Father with great hurt. Both have forced him to trust in his heavenly Father completely when he has no answers. He says that in the pain and the confusion

---

14 Ed Shaw, *Purposeful Sexuality: A Short Christian Introduction* (IVP, 2021), p 29.

there has been such blessing in his life and in the lives of others. Perhaps you can relate to his story.

You cannot control your children's sexuality. You cannot determine if they will spend their lives married or single. You can teach them the goodness of God, the truthfulness of his word, and the goodness of both marriage and singleness. You can encourage them not to label themselves too early when their feelings may change. It is not helpful to have an elaborate "coming out" ceremony for their peer group. It *is* helpful for them to take the time to learn about themselves with those godly people they trust. You can help them to see that feelings can change but that they might not. Ed says that his haven't—but his family and friends loved him just the same, always encouraging him in his faith as the priority. His identity is defined by Christ's love for him, not by who he finds attractive.

I know a young woman at church who was advised by her friends at school to "come out" as heterosexual (yes, you read that right). They said it was time everyone knew. Wisely, she doesn't see that its anyone else's business. Her sexuality and her desires are hers alone. For the moment she is single. She is clear that her decisions each day are determined by her faith in Christ, not by who she finds most attractive in the school corridors.

Whether they are same-sex-attracted or not, single friends can have a valuable role in our families just as we can have valuable one in theirs. Our brilliant single friends are fabulous role models for my children. They are living proof that you don't need to marry or be sexually active to be happy and fulfilled (just like Jesus)—that what we need is simply friends. Encourage your kids to dream just as much about the great days they will spend with friends as they might dream about their wedding. We don't all need a spouse, and we're not promised one. We do all need friends.

And we do all need to remember that what our kids most need is Jesus. Worrying about whether they'll be same-sex-attracted, or whether they'll get married, or whether they'll have kids might be a sign that we're more concerned with their worldly happiness and our worldly dreams (because, deep down, we all want grandchildren one day) than with the eternal health of their souls. Worrying about whether the culture will corrupt them might be a sign that we're underestimating the power of God's Spirit to save and sustain them. But if we're convinced of the goodness of Jesus and the power of his Spirit, then we'll probably do a decent job if one day we're chopping vegetables in the kitchen and one of our kids says, "Mum... Dad... I think I might be..."

Questions to think about...

1. Think about your child's experience with their friends. How can you best help them to be godly in their friendships?

2. Have you been able to bring a diversity of family friends, including married and unmarried people, into your home? Are there steps you can take to do this more?

3. Do you feel able to present the biblical model for marriage and the goodness of singleness in a compelling, inspiring way to your child?

4. Has the topic of sexuality already been raised in your family? How did it go? Would you approach it differently next time?

9

BOYS, GIRLS AND GENDER

A friend of mine recently preached four sermons at his church on gender. He found that *all* the parents wanted their teenagers in for the sermons when normally they would be in a youth group next door. When it comes to gender, we know that things have moved fast, and we know we need help.

Matt started one sermon by asking everyone to raise their hand if they agreed with the statement "Men and women are different". Almost all the hands went up. Simple. He then asked everyone to imagine the beginning of their answer to the question "How are men and women different?" There was a careful silence. Cheeks were chewed. Deep breaths. Not so simple.

As I said, we know that things have moved fast, and we know we need help.

MALE AND FEMALE HE CREATED THEM

Let's return to where we've so often been in this book: to the very beginning...

> *So God created mankind in his own image,*
> *in the image of God he created them;*
> *male and female he created them. (Genesis 1:27)*

As we've seen, you and I are the main event in creation, created in the image of God. Above all else, we must take away that we are the pinnacle of creation because we are made "in his own image". We are *like him*, in a way that nothing else is.

If you were writing Genesis, after the making of image-bearing humanity, what would you choose to highlight about what humanity is like? Coming from an engineering background, I would want to mention opposable thumbs, massive brains and our unique ability to form spoken words. Perhaps you are more cultured and interesting than me, and you want to highlight the ability to make music, the exploration of our planet or the invention of the flushing toilet. But none of those is where the Spirit-inspired author went. The only distinctive mentioned is that we are created male and female.

That seems strange when we consider that presumably every other kind of animal, bird and fish was also created male and female. There are two headlines in the story of our creation.

1. We are created in God's image to relate to him. We are made to relate to him.

2. We are each male or female. We are made to relate to one another.

It is not a long list. To be male or female is who we are. It comes second only to being created in the image of the omnipotent divine being. It is a privilege and honour to be made male or female by our Creator. He has judged it to be significant—it is at the heart of who we are. We can tell our children that the Lord delights in their boy-ness or their girl-ness.

BOY OR GIRL

In this cultural moment, we in the West seem to be working hard to eliminate the differences between men and women. That will affect our parenting. Many of us find ourselves trying to raise our children as "children", not as "boys" and "girls". Much of that is because we are still learning how to fix the mistakes of past sexism. Throughout most of our history, and in much of the world today, girls have not been treated as the equals of boys that their creation demands. The Bible has consistently been countercultural in the equality and recognition it has given to women, most clearly seen in how Jesus acted. It is Christians who can be clearest that there must be equality between the sexes.

There is an ongoing conversation happening about men's and women's distinctive roles in marriage and church leadership. That's not really our concern here because we're talking about *boys and girls*. What do Christian parents need to say about being a boy and being a girl?

First, and most simply, each child is a boy or a girl. Their body tells them, and everyone else, which they are. The Bible speaks of God handcrafting each of our bodies (see chapter 7). He made each body either male or female. You can see which.

Those conversations start early. Most parents have had very peculiar conversations with their young children when either parent or child or both were not wearing clothes. For a time, one friend lived in fear of his daughters discussing his body (in great detail) at school, as he felt they talked about little else at home. I know another friend whose son *did* discuss his father's body in the most intimate, proud terms at school. That's not a subject any of us want to have our child's teacher raise at parents' evening!

We teach our children that there is an age when we should not be naked in front of others and that there are some conversations that we have with only very few people— and that, as they grow, those conversations are ones that we, as their parents, will want to have with them. We start the conversation and stand ready to continue it as it develops, in a way that shows we delight in the biological differences and the countless similarities. As always, our tone and manner teaches them so much. Their bodies are beautiful. They keep a few parts hidden because they are precious, not because they are shameful or ugly.

You never know when the opportunity for these kinds of conversations will come up (or be forced on you). I was on a church weekend away, delighted that my 5-year-old son had got involved in a pop-up sports match. I was having a conversation on the sidelines. It was all going so well. Time with our church family should be like this! Then I glanced over to see my son dropping his shorts and the other children gathering around, all looking at his underwear. Everyone was laughing, including my son. To this day I have no idea how sport turned into that. I also have no idea what was going to happen next. I do know that my son was having a great time.

I ran over and tried to persuade everyone to get back to the sport rather than engage with this new pastime. I explained to my son (again) that everything inside his underwear is precious and not to be shared or shown to others; even his underwear should be kept covered.

These are important messages for our children before they are out of our direct care (at school or at friends' houses). We need them to understand at an early age that others do not get to see or touch those areas. It is good to tell them clearly that they should not allow others to do that and that they can talk to us about any situations in which it might happen.

Our bodies have been made crafted beautifully, and we thank God for them as a unique gift given individually to us. That is the starting point in understanding what it means to be a boy or a girl. God has chosen which we are, and given us that body as a good gift, and so we thank him for the distinctives of our gendered body, because if he chose and made them, wonderfully and fearfully, then we can learn to share his delight in his handiwork.

STEREOTYPES, TRENDS AND GODLINESS

Unhealthy gender stereotypes tell us that children's bodies must be used in certain ways: girls do craft and boys play football; girls are emotional and boys are methodical. And there can be a corner of Christian culture that places a burden on boys and girls that the Bible does not. In reality, the girl who loves rugby and never wears a dress is not a tomboy; she is just a girl who likes playing sport in a tracksuit.

In 1 Thessalonians 2, Paul reminds the church in Thessalonica of how he and his team conducted his ministry among them:

> *Just as a nursing mother cares for her children, so we cared for you. Because we loved you so much, we were delighted to share with you not only the gospel of God but our lives as well. (1 Thessalonians 2:7-8)*

Mothers often care for their baby in this way. They love their child by sharing every moment of their day (and much of the night) with them. There is something distinctly motherly about the way a woman cares for her baby. And yet Paul, a single man without any children of his own, was happy to be motherly in the way he treated others. We can make a general observation about the way that women often care for others, seen most clearly in motherhood. But some men will be like this, and Paul chose to be like this. Yet he also says that he was like a father:

> *For you know that we dealt with each of you as a father deals with his own children, encouraging, comforting and*

urging you to live lives worthy of God, who calls you into his kingdom and glory. (v 11-12)

Fathers often encourage, comfort and urge on their children. They spur their children on, showing them how to persevere, pressing on to the goal. There is something distinctively fatherly about the way a father encourages his children. And yet Paul, a man without children, was happy to say that he pastored others as a father. So Paul identifies a general way that men encourage others, seen most clearly in fatherhood. Yet some women will be like this, and it is great for them to encourage others in this way.

My children complain whenever we go for walks (which is awkward, as it is what we do most days on holiday). My wife and I adopt these two different roles on those walks. It's usually me who has the plan and the route in mind. I try to stay enthusiastic, whispering in the ears of my elder two to stay upbeat for the sake of our youngest. Sometimes I have carried a sleeping bundle on my back or held the hand of the most tired when it has turned out that my plan is utterly impractical. My wife has the bag of snacks and spare gloves. She listens more carefully to their groans, informing me when they are actually tired (rather than just complaining that we should have taken the car). We didn't plan it this way. Most men and women seem to follow these trends. But if we saw parents doing it the other way round, they would not be doing it wrong or being less godly. Of most importance in Paul's descriptions of motherhood and fatherhood is that both parents place the needs of their children before their own.

We can say, then, that God has made men and women in such a way that they tend towards particular characteristics. Girls generally seem to be better at communicating—at engaging well with others in order to understand their needs.[15] This does not mean we should raise all girls to be in caring professions, like teaching and medical roles. It is right for *all* children to learn that whatever gifting they have, they should follow Christ in using their gift to serve the needs of others above their own needs. But still, the data points to this particular gifting being generally more prevalent in girls.

We can also say that God has made men and women generally different physically. For instance, after puberty boys' bodies are usually stronger than girls' bodies.[16] We do not need to raise all boys believing that godly men must be strong warriors or assertive leaders. That would be to force boys to fit a model that is more cultural than biblical. It is right for *all* children to learn that whatever strength or advantage they have, they should follow Christ in using it to protect those more vulnerable than themselves. But still, the data points to physical strength being generally more prevalent in boys.

Bridger Walker was only six years old when he put himself between a vicious dog and his younger sister. While the dog was attacking him, he told her to run away. When he

---

15 https://blogs.scientificamerican.com/beautiful-minds/taking-sex-differences-in-personality-seriously (accessed December 5th, 2022).

16 https://www.livescience.com/33513-men-vs-women-our-physical-differences-explained.html (accessed December 5th, 2022).

managed to escape the dog, he immediately ran to her and took her to a place of safety. He needed 90 stitches in his head following the attack. When his family asked him afterwards why he did it, he replied, "If someone had to die, I thought it should be me".

Even when a boy's physical frame is small, it is a God-given instinct in him to use whatever strength he has to serve, protect and care for others. Godliness is seeking to understand how God has prepared us for acts of service (Ephesians 2:10).

The difference in trends between men and women in general is why I had different conversations with my teenage son and daughter after we watched a recent documentary that highlighted the widespread low-level sexual abuse of teenage girls in secondary schools by boys. I wanted my son to see that, as a man, he is more likely to be stronger and more likely to be aroused by what he sees. He needs to know this about men so that he can fight his (likely) temptation and use the strength he will (probably) have to protect women. I wanted my daughter to know that widespread bad behaviour never makes it acceptable. She needs to learn how to speak up for herself and others. It takes courage to speak up for yourself and others when you feel vulnerable.

In all this, we need to be careful not to push too far. There are plenty of men who are smaller or less strong than some women, but they are no are less male or godly. There are plenty of women who are less emotionally attuned to others' needs than some men, and they are no less female or godly for it. We raise our sons and daughters to be godly.

GENDER IDENTITY

Every cell of our bodies is either male or female. Our sex is more than skin deep. It is not just limited to which genitals we have. God has created us to be thoroughly one sex or another.[17] There is a "givenness" about our sex— and so there is "givenness" about our gender, for our sex tells us what gender we are. And that stands against the current phenomenon of gender identity, which proclaims that we can choose which gender we are based on which gender we feel we are.

Your "sex" is biological and unchangeable, based on chromosomes, hormones and genitals; culturally speaking, your "gender" has come to mean how you express your sex. This gender expression will vary according to your culture (in 18th-century Scotland, men wore skirts. In 20th-century France, they really didn't.) Contrary to the biblical view, our culture today says that your gender identity can be chosen by you, not given to you by God. Your choice, we are told, is based on your subjective, internal sense of being a man or woman or another category altogether, rather than being derived necessarily from your biological sex. To experience gender dysphoria

---

17 That is not to forget that some people are born intersex. As Andrew Walker says in *God and the Transgender Debate*, "To think in biblical language, what we are seeing here is an aspect of creation that has been marred by the fall—a deviation from a norm that reaffirms that a norm exists in the first place" (The Good Book Company, 2022), p 166.

is to feel that you have a different gender identity to your sex. The complex question that follows is whether those with this felt misalignment of gender and sex should be helped to change (or understand) their internal sense, or to change their appearance or bodies so that they present as the gender they feel.

There is currently a narrative that this inner conflict between sex and gender has always existed, with the only difference now being that today there is an openness to letting people express themselves "properly". But there is another perspective. There have always been a number of pre-pubescent children (mostly boys) who did not feel that they fitted into the cultural stereotypes. Perhaps those boys like to play in dresses, wear pink or play with glitter. It is ok for a boy to be different to other boys. He can play and pursue pastimes as he enjoys them or is gifted at them. He is still a boy. It is also normal for children, as they grow up, to play at being the opposite sex, as a way of exploring gender differences. The right response to this is neither to panic and prevent them doing so nor to jump to the conclusion that they are in "the wrong body". We need to leave them to play and to help them to enjoy the bodies God has given them.

Studies show that the vast majority of children who want to be the opposite gender will become comfortable with their biological sex after puberty.[18] The recent promotion of the view that these children are transgender prompts them to

---

18 https://www.ncbi.nlm.nih.gov/pmc/articles/PMC5841333/ (accessed December 5th, 2022).

question their gender, encouraging them to take seriously the notion that they could and should change their gender. This is deeply unhelpful. Our role as parents, particularly with younger children, is to provide the certainty that their body is a good gift that cannot be changed, and that (within the limits of physics) they can use their bodies for whatever adventures they can imagine. They should not think that their gender should limit their hobbies, friendships, sports or aspirations for the future.

Post-puberty, around three-quarters of teenagers today who want to identify as the opposite gender are girls. The question should be asked: why is this? A common story is that of a teenage girl who doesn't feel like she fits in. She is constantly presented with a cultural image of women as being perfectly manicured sexual objects, and quite reasonably she doesn't want to be part of that story. Such girls might get involved with an LGBT club at school, where they feel accepted and loved. The appeal of transitioning is reinforced by spending time online watching stories of those who say that transitioning has made them feel more comfortable.

It is a rare teenager who always likes their body and wouldn't consider some way of "opting out" of who they are and how they feel. However, instead of encouraging them to talk through their concerns in a trusted relationship, identifying as transgender and/or transitioning is being held out as a way to escape these feelings, in a similar way to self-harm. (The difference is that no healthcare professionals advocate self-harm.) In a culture in which our young people are being told that they should not suffer and that there is always an escape from uncomfortable feelings, then they may well take hold of whatever solution is offered.

It is intimidating and bewildering to be a parent in this fast-changing culture. But while this specific situation may be new, parenting unhappy and confused teenagers is as old as the hills. There have been plenty of generations before us whose teenagers have had to live through greater trauma and distress than ours. In God we have a rock—an unshifting solid and secure foundation on which to build our lives. Every storm and turbulence in our children's lives is an opportunity to invite them to stand on the rock next to us. Often it is in fear and confusion that Christ's lordship can be experienced and understood most clearly. Let us tell our children that Christ is the one and only unchanging feature of our lives. Let us also be honest enough to explain that it is normal to feel uncertain about other aspects of our lives, including changing bodies and new feelings, which we navigate alongside the shifting sands of friendships.

It is tempting to place issues like sexuality and gender into a box marked, "Frightening. New. Jesus Christ can't help." Instead we can be certain that, as with all issues, Jesus Christ is enough for us, that the Bible offers us all the wisdom we need, and that his Spirit is at work as we listen, pray and talk through the concerns. We know our children best, so we are the right people to navigate through this with them. They may think they should be listening to the beautiful, reassuring faces on Instagram. Our love and patience can convince them they are wrong.

Do not believe the lie that the most loving way forward is to do what the child wants. God did not do that with us! He knew best. He loved us by telling us we had gone wrong. He brought us home. As parents, we have been placed in our children's lives to show them that journey. You are equipped to do this.

Very often, those who are seeking medical help to change their gender have pre-existing mental illness, are on the autistic spectrum, have been through trauma, or have cut themselves off from others, spending more and more time online. Gender identity has become their lifeboat in the storm. Those who love them can get them out, into creation, doing activities that remind them of the joy available to them. They can start to show them, and talk to them about, the bigger story of their identity.

It is striking that this issue is dominated by the idea that children must be allowed to determine who they are, based on how they feel. Young people are being told that instead of looking at their body to determine their gender they should look within themselves to discover their gender.

Leaving our children to discern their identity from their inner selves is to leave them in a situation that is unstable, uncertain and even arbitrary. We need instead to show them who God says they are, how God has made them, and who God calls them to become. The more we tell the positive story to our kids—that they are made by a great God and loved by a great Saviour—the more they'll be confident in who they have been made and redeemed to be, even when life feels difficult or their bodies feel strange; and the easier it will be to talk with them, gently but clearly, about the lies that underpin the transgender movement.

None of this is easy. It should drive us to prayer. It should cause us to support one another in our churches. But it should not drive us to blind panic. Jesus is not surprised or defeated by the 21st century, and his people needn't be either.

Questions to think about...

1. How could your parenting be influenced by unhelpful gender stereotypes?

2. Do you feel able to offer your child a better story for those who feel like they want to be the other gender to their own?

3. How would you answer the question, "How are men and women different?"

10

WITH JESUS, LIKE JESUS

Danny is 8 years old. He loves playing with Lego and spending time with his family. His dad loves the sea, so he takes him out on his paddleboard whenever he can. He usually sits next to his mum in church and engages attentively.

Danny has Duchenne muscular dystrophy. It is marked by progressive muscle degeneration, and it is life-limiting. As he gets older, Danny is losing abilities that he learnt when he was younger. At the moment, he finds walking difficult and struggles to stand up on his own to sing in church. His parents expect him to need a wheelchair by his early teens and eventually to need a machine to help him to breathe. People with Danny's condition usually have their lifespan considerably shortened. We interviewed his parents for our podcast. I wept during our preparatory conversation beforehand. I suspect you will have found these paragraphs hard to read.

Danny's mum has got to know other parents whose children have the same disease. They share what she describes as "chronic sadness"—a constant daily ache and hurt that doesn't pass. A difference she sees between herself and them, though, is that most parents have a great drive to be involved in fundraising for research into a cure. Danny's mum would love there to be a cure—she has campaigned for the provision of drugs to relieve his symptoms and slow the progression of the disease. But her greatest drive is for her son to be certain that he is heading for the new creation, where all pain will pass away, all tears will stop, and he will run freely and enjoy the very best life, without end. Danny's mum's greatest hope is that Danny will keep trusting in Jesus.

Danny's dad told me that he thinks about the resurrection every day. Before being a parent, he understood the resurrection, but he didn't hold tight to it daily. Now he can't imagine how he could go on without it. Most of their parenting looks beautifully like the biblical model we have been thinking about together in the pages of this book. They provide loving boundaries to Danny's behaviour. They try to be fair in how they treat him and his sister. They take him to school and pick him up from school. They invite people into their home and encourage him in his friendships. And they take opportunities to point out his identity as a loved child of God and to look forward together to his future in the new creation.

What is so striking to me about Danny's story is that his disease means his parents really are thinking daily about the new creation. It affects their thoughts, their feelings and their parenting. It comforts them and spurs them on. They are clear that their great goal and desperate prayer is for their son to know Jesus Christ as his Lord every day of his life. His disease means they don't get distracted from this purpose by the temptations, idols and plain busyness of parenting. Instead they parent for Danny's eternity.

My children are healthy and have no disease. But they do have a life-limiting condition. They will one day die. Their days are numbered. God knows the exact number of the days of their life, and I do not (Job 14:5). That should motivate me to be as clear and deliberate in my parenting as Danny's parents are. While my children's days in this life will likely be more numerous than Danny's, they will not be without end, and I would love to have that same clear-minded urgency for their eternity.

LIKE HIM

As parents, we tend to want to fix our children. Most of us accepted a long time ago that we don't have a family of all-round winners, but we had hoped for "average" or even "a bit special in some ways". We can find ourselves wishing for "normal". In chapter 5 we held tight to the hope that our children are a work in progress. The Spirit is not done with them; indeed, we have the promise that for those who put their trust in Christ, he who began this good work in them will carry it on to completion (Philippians 1:6). But (and no parent wants to read this "But"), we have no promise that every struggle, every sadness and every cause of anguish will be eliminated soon. The evidence I have for this is my own life. I am not totally fixed. There are huge parts of my life where I am far below where I desire to be.

Life remains hard. Danny's situation is hard for him and his parents. While we believe in a supernatural God who can do absolutely anything, Christians have not been promised that every disability or cause of struggle will be healed this side of the new creation. I suspect that if you thought about it for a few seconds, you could come up with some aspect of your children's lives, character or gifting that you expect to make their lives a little more difficult. The causes are as varied as there are people. Disability, illness and mental-health struggles can follow people through life. Getting older can make these worse, not better. Some aspects of character, gifting, sexuality or marital status can make life feel harder. Grief, hurt and regret can feel like a shadow for many years. Jesus can bring healing and redemption to many of these areas, but even then there are often scars (not just physical ones) that remain. To be a Christian is to know that it is in our weakness that we see most clearly the strength of the one we follow (2 Corinthians 12:9). One benefit of this perspective is that we need not be afraid of admitting where we are struggling or that our child has a weakness or struggle. Indeed, we believe that God will always use that weakness in the life of the Christian for their good (Romans 8:28). These are wonderful promises; but they do not change the "chronic sadness" in the hard situations that life brings.

Yet we are never without hope. We really can be "sorrowful, yet always rejoicing" (2 Corinthians 6:10)—about our children as well as about ourselves. As Christians, whatever our struggle, however inevitable the future feels, there is an eventual better, final story. The promise of the new creation for all those who trust in Christ is not only a promise for where we will be but who we will be. We will be like Jesus. And if we know who we will be, then we can live through our todays:

> *See what great love the Father has lavished on us, that we should be called children of God! And that is what we are! The reason the world does not know us is that it did not know him. Dear friends, now we are children of God, and what we will be has not yet been made known. But we know that when Christ appears, we shall be like him, for we shall see him as he is. (1 John 3:1-2)*

We have seen this first verse before. Those two exclamation marks shout to us that our faith gives us our identity. We are children of God! But as we read on, we discover what we will be, or rather who we will be. "We shall be like him." Pause to drink that in. I can't really imagine it. Right now, though I am being made a little more like Jesus with each passing year, I am also more and more aware of how far there still is to go. Right now, I try to live a life of worship of my Lord. I persevere. I push on. I falter. I get up again. You and I are not like Jesus. But one day, we will be. We will see him in all his glory and love and kindness and patience, and in that moment, we will see that we've become like him.

We will love like he loves. Sin and death will be conquered. Our struggles will be over. Our doubts will vanish. That is what John is telling us in those verses. He is calling us to lift our eyes beyond the current hurt, struggle and frustration of our lives and of our parenting—to fix our gaze on our certain final identity.

LOOK FORWARD

There is a running route I like to take when I visit my parents-in-law. They live on a hill beside a disused railway that still has its rails and its rotting sleepers (ties, if you're American) in place. On either side is a ditch and slippery mud. The first part of my run is along that railway, and I have to watch every step I take. Some sleepers are too rotten to step on. I have to stride long and short to not twist an ankle. It's difficult. It's exhausting. It's barely running. When I make the turn, I leave the railway and run back along the road, up the hill. It's still tiring, but now I can see the house. The road is straight and the tarmac is trustworthy. My destination is on the horizon. I don't have to look at my feet. The distance to home is decreasing. My pace picks up. It's hard, but I can see where I'm heading, and I know I will make it.

It is possible to parent while looking only at our feet. The struggle, the hurt and the mess always seem to be under our feet. Each step has to be measured. We constantly feel like we are about to trip up (or have just tripped up). It's exhausting, and it frequently feels like we can't go the distance.

Look forward. Parent by keeping your eyes fixed on our destination. It doesn't fix everything. The hurt is still there. But you can keep going. Your perspective on your current situation is changed by the certainty of the destination. If you are trusting Jesus, you shall be like him, for you shall see him as he is.

I would run through brick walls for that moment. And what is more, I would run through brick walls for my children if I thought it would get them there. So, I tell them about it, and I invite them to run towards it with me. I tell them that Jesus loves them, and died and rose again so that they can be with him, and be like him, one day.

A child's timescale is generally tiny. At the start of December, Christmas Day still seems years away. Teenagers struggle to remember about the future—I am told that a part of the teenage experience is the struggle to consider consequences because their brains focus far too much on the moment. Bad decisions get made for the thrill of the immediate high. The consequences that follow come as a shock. Fear of missing out (FOMO) is the driving force, and fear of consequences is totally non-existent.

God's timescale, on the other hand, is absolutely massive. It stretches out eternally. Our children need their parents to lift their glance from time to time and point them to the horizon. It might be when they, or their family, are in the bottom of the lowest pit, or it might be as you stand and look at the horizon on a beach or from the top of a hill. Look forward yourself, and invite them to do so with you.

ONE DAY...

I'm writing days before I am due to attend a funeral with my children for someone they loved dearly. I have spent recent days talking to them about what to expect of the funeral: the sadness for those left behind, the tears that will flow, and the deep ache to be with the person again. We have also been talking about our Christian hope of life after death, as well as the sadness of dying without that Christian hope and the eternal consequences. These are not conversations we often have. Though the situation is heartbreaking, I am grateful for the chance to be talking about the biggest advert for being a Christian.

A friend raised her children in Nigeria. Death was a part of everyday conversation there. Chickens would be slaughtered on the doorstep, to be cooked for dinner. People died, and the community discussed it. Death happened around her children. It was also a more Christianised culture, so death, heaven and hell were topics of conversations between friends and neighbours. She did not need to choose to discuss it with her children; it just happened. In the West, though, we have banished death from our lives. I am in my mid 40s, and I am yet to see a dead body. That would be impossible in most other times and places. Our schools don't mention death. Our media don't deal with it. Social media resorts to easy clichés to discuss it. Our children feel immortal.

Let us not go along with this lie. Death is real and inevitable and tragic. The Christian hope is that there is a cure for death. With the yes of faith, we can see our home on the horizon: life beyond death. One day, our identity as children of God will be seen. It will be certain. It will be proved with our senses. We will see it, touch it and even taste it as we sit at the banquet with Jesus. We shall be like him, for we shall see him as he is.

THE FINAL GOAL OF PARENTING

We are given a vision of the moment when we will stand before the throne of Christ in the new creation.

> *After this I looked, and there before me was a great multitude that no one could count, from every nation, tribe, people and language, standing before the throne and before the Lamb. They were wearing white robes and were holding palm branches in their hands. And they cried out in a loud voice:*
>
> *"Salvation belongs to our God,*
> *who sits on the throne,*
> *and to the Lamb." (Revelation 7:9-10)*

Imagine standing in that crowd, lost in ecstasy. This is better than being in the front row for the ultimate music gig of your favourite band, better than rising for the standing ovation at the curtain call for the greatest play, better than the moment in extra time when the winning goal is scored for your team in the cup final. The great prayer of parenting is that standing next to you in this final, wonderful multitude is your child. The age gap has disappeared. Instead of parent and child, you are now brothers and sisters. I can't see how I won't weep with joy in that moment. I imagine placing my hand on my childrens' shoulders and squeezing, just enough so that they glance over to me, allowing me a moment of eye contact and a broad smile. All past arguments, failures and frustrations will be forgotten forever. Our journey will be over. Our destination will be reached. Our eternity will be wonderful.

We parent for that privilege. It is not in our hands. But we can pray for it. We can strive for it. We can point our kids towards it. We can show them and we can say to them that there is a loving heavenly Father who loves them more even than we do, and who invites them to put their faith in Jesus and walk through this life confidently, because they know where they are heading; they know that one day everything will be ok; they know that they are children of God who one day will see Jesus and be like Jesus.

Questions to think about...

1. What is making you feel sorrowful at the moment? Are there reasons for thankfulness even in those hard parts of life?

2. What aspects of the new creation are you most looking forward to?

3. When could you imagine the new creation being mentioned in family conversations?

4. Since this is the last chapter of this book, as you look back on all you've read...

   - what has most encouraged you about your parenting? (Make sure you name at least one thing.)

   - what would you most like to change in your parenting? (Be specific.)

   - what do you need to think more about?

   - what aspect of the gospel have you been most excited or comforted by?

Raising Confident Kids in a Confusing World is part of a package of resources created to equip churches and parents to raise children who understand their God-given identity.

WHO AM i?

The Who am I? Foundation Course is a 7-week resource for churches to use with 4-11 year olds. It comes with leaders' study notes, all-age talks, Sunday School lesson plans and parents' handouts. Available as a **FREE** download from **www.faithinkids.org**.

The Kids' podcasts are 20 minutes of engaging joy for the whole family. 7 episodes to dovetail with the Foundation Course.

The Parents' podcasts bring experts into the conversation to equip parents for the biggest conversations with their children.

Search 'faithinkids podcast' for both of these.

faith(in)kids

Going futher! Church resources covering sexuality, pornography, gender identity and body image for over 8 year olds.

COMING SOON

faith in kids

exists to see confident parents and thriving churches raising children together to trust Jesus eternally.

We do this by encouraging, inspiring and equipping the influencers of faith in children with support, training and resources.

Parents, kids ministry leaders and church leaders; why not check out our **FREE** resources here: **www.faithinkids.org**

Or connect with us here:

Ed Drew, the author of this book, is also the Director of Ministry at Faith in Kids

You've got this!

thegoodbook
COMPANY

BIBLICAL | RELEVANT | ACCESSIBLE

At The Good Book Company, we are dedicated to helping Christians and local churches grow. We believe that God's growth process always starts with hearing clearly what he has said to us through his timeless word—the Bible.

Ever since we opened our doors in 1991, we have been striving to produce Bible-based resources that bring glory to God. We have grown to become an international provider of user-friendly resources to the Christian community, with believers of all backgrounds and denominations using our books, Bible studies, devotionals, evangelistic resources, and DVD-based courses.

We want to equip ordinary Christians to live for Christ day by day, and churches to grow in their knowledge of God, their love for one another, and the effectiveness of their outreach.

Call us for a discussion of your needs or visit one of our local websites for more information on the resources and services we provide.

Your friends at The Good Book Company

thegoodbook.com | thegoodbook.co.uk
thegoodbook.com.au | thegoodbook.co.nz
thegoodbook.co.in